Physical Characteristics of the Pomeranian

(from the American Kennel Club breed standard)

Back: Short with a level topline; compact and well-ribbed with brisket reaching the elbow.

Tail: Plumed, lies flat and straight on the back.

Hindquarters: The angulation of the hindquarters balances that of the forequarters. The thighs are moderately muscled with stifles that are moderately bent and clearly defined.

Coat: Double. The undercoat is soft and dense. The outer coat is long, straight, glistening and harsh in texture.

Hindlegs: Straight and parallel to each other.

Size: The average weight of the Pomeranian is from 3 to 7 pounds, with the ideal weight for the show specimen being 4 to 6 pounds.

Feet: Well-arched, compact, and turn neither in nor out. He stands well up on his toes.

Pomeranian

◇

by Juliette Cunliffe

Contents

KENNEL CLUB BOOKS® POMERANIAN
ISBN: 1-59378-252-7

Copyright © 2003, **2005** • Kennel Club Books, LLC
308 Main Street, Allenhurst, NJ 07711 USA
Cover Design Patented: US 6,435,559 B2 • Printed in South Korea

PHOTO CREDITS:
Norvia Behling, T. J. Calhoun, Carolina Biological Supply, Doskocil, Isabelle Français, James Hayden-Yoav, James R. Hayden, Carol Ann Johnson, Bill Jonas, Dwight R. Kuhn, Dr. Dennis Kunkel, Mikki Pet Products, Antonio Philippe, Phototake, RBP, Jean Claude Revy, Dr. Andrew Spielman, Alice van Kempen and C. James Webb.
Illustrations by Patricia Peters.

The publisher would like to thank Averil Cawthera-Purdy, Dorothy Entwistle, Stacy MacDonald, Robert Morris, Mario J. Panlilio, Jr. and the rest of the owners of the dogs featured in this book.

Today's tiny Pomeranian derives from the large spitz breeds of Germany. Our modern dog is a fashionable and petite member of the Toy Group.

HISTORY OF THE

POMERANIAN

Although now well known as one of the smallest of the Toy breeds, the Pomeranian was formerly considerably larger. Those unfamiliar with the breed will probably be surprised by some of the early paintings of Pomeranians, for the dogs shown look large by today's standards, sitting alongside their elegant mistresses.

THE BREED'S NAME
The breed's name derives from its homeland of Pomerania, a former duchy on the Baltic, between eastern Germany and western Poland. The Pomeranian was a descendant of European working dogs. Such dogs were also held in high esteem in Greece and Rome, where they were prized as ladies' pets. In classical Grecian times, the Pomeranian was called the "Maltese Dog," which has on occasion led to some confusion.

The earliest record of the name "Pomeranian" is found in *Voyage of Discovery Around the World*, written by George Vancouver. He reported that on May 24, 1792, he had visited an Indian village where he had found a number of dogs "resembling those of Pomerania, though somewhat larger." They were, he said,

The Deutscher Kleinspitz, the smallest of the German Spitz breeds, resembles the Pomeranian, and in some places is still regarded as the same breed.

shaven close to the skin and the people had clothing and blankets made from their coats.

The Deutscher Grossspitz, one of the largest of the German Spitz breeds, resembles the Pomeranian in coat and type but stands 16 inches tall.

EARLY USE

Dogs of this kind were originally used mainly to control sheep and cattle, as well as to round up reindeer. They were known generally as Wolfspitz dogs and lie behind the Pomeranians, Schipperkes, German Spitzen, Samoyeds, Norwegian Elkhounds and Keeshonden we know today. Other names by which the breed's ancestors were known were Fox-

The Pomeranian's popularity in the America and UK has precluded the advancement of the German Kleinspitz in those countries.

dog, Spitz-dog and Loup-Loup. Indeed one of the animals from which they offered protection for the flocks was the wolf, and it was said that such dogs never failed to attack with success!

The Pomeranian not only was known in Western Europe but also was used in the cold wastelands of Russia and Siberia to pull sledges. Russia's Laika, a dog known by many for its employ in

space travel, also has similar ancestry to that of the Pomeranian. Indeed it is generally accepted that the Pomeranian derives from one of the northern Arctic spitz breeds. The Samoyed, found in Siberia along the shores of the Arctic Ocean, and the large white Pomeranian found earlier in Britain bore many similarities.

FASCINATING DESCRIPTION

By the turn of the 20th century the Pomeranian was, however, a different dog in many ways.

Certainly it was no longer pulling sledges or herding sheep. By way of introduction to the breed, Herbert Compton's description of the Pomeranian makes fascinating reading: "We weigh about 6 lb as a rule, and the only mutton we take care of is roasted, and on a plate. Moreover, the modern Pom, in conformity with the fashionable circles it has entered, has elaborated its wardrobe, and you shall find it wearing coats of many colors, to wit—white, black, gray, fawn, red, blue, chocolate, brown, beaver, sable, orange and parti-colored. Like a star-rocket, it has ascended aloft and burst into many tints, and very, very small splashes of them. It is no longer Brobdingnangian and blood-thirsting for the wolf, but Lilliputian and addicted to the lap. Moreover it has learned good manners and ceased to labor under the imputa-

FROM WOLF TO WOLFSPITZ

Dogs and wolves are members of the genus *Canis*. Wolves are known scientifically as *Canis lupus* while dogs are known as *Canis domesticus*. Dogs and wolves are known to interbreed. The term *canine* derives from the Latin-derived word *Canis*. The term *dog* has no scientific basis but has been used for thousands of years. The origin of the word *dog* has never been authoritatively ascertained.

tion of being snappish, untrustworthy and dangerous to children, as was its character not so long ago, being deemed affectionate, gentle and well-behaved. It has but to moderate the rancor of its tongue—in other words, to be less feverishly noisy—to become in every way a pattern for pet-dogs."

COLOR

The colors of the Pomeranian are wide-ranging and it seems that, in the past, several of the European countries specialized in different colors. The white Pomeranian was a native of France, while the red is believed to have come from Italy. Although black and white Pomeranians were to be found in the 19th century, these were seemingly rarely good specimens of the breed, creams and reds being the more popular colors then. In the 1880s, it was said that

The Schipperke of Belgium also derives from the spitz family of dogs. The breed is usually seen in solid black, though other colors such as fawn and cream also occur.

MEET THE SPITZEN

The Pomeranian derives from the family of dogs we know today as the German Spitzen, of which five breeds are recognized by Europe's Fédération Cynologique Internationale (FCI). The largest of these is the German Wolfspitz, standing 18 in and possessing the characteristic spitz coat in a wolf gray coloration. The Deutscher Grossspitz, sometimes called the Giant or Great Spitz, stands at least 16 in and can be colored in any solid color. The Deutscher Mittelspitz (Standard), standing about 14 in; Kleinspitz (Small or Miniature), standing about 11 in; and Zwergspitz (Toy), standing about 8 in, complete the family. The Kleinspitz has retained the appellation Victorian Pomeranian, and the Zwergspitz is identical to the Pomeranian in size.

the breed in Britain was practically confined to white Pomeranians, their weight in the region of 9 kg (20 lb). However, from the author Dalziel, we learn that there was a strain of rich fawns kept in the neighborhood of Birmingham about 1860.

In 1911, the first orange Pomeranian in Britain was Offley Henry Drew who, mated to Eng. Ch. Mars, set the foundation for the orange color that was to become so popular. Not until the 1930s did a wide range of uniform colors become available in Britain, with orange becoming an especially fashionable color during the 20th century. Whites are now only seen occasionally, but blacks seem to have had something of a revival in the last twenty years.

SIZE

Ancestors of today's Pomeranian were considerably larger than this diminutive breed that now weighs only 4–5.5 lb. Some of these early dogs weighed as much as 40–50 lb, but size has been carefully bred down during the last 200 years or so. Queen Victoria's dogs weighed on average around 2.7 lb.

EARLY INTEREST IN BRITAIN

Queen Charlotte, who was the German wife of King George III, brought a pair of Pomeranians to Britain in 1767. Their names were Phoebe (also spelt Phebe) and Mercury. They lived in Kew in

West London, as did the artist Sir Thomas Gainsborough, thus many paintings of these royal dogs are to be found.

In 1870, the English Kennel Club officially recognized the Pomeranian as the "Spitzdog." The breed was brought to the attention of Britain's public when Queen Victoria became interested in the Pomeranian. Despite being Queen Charlotte's granddaughter, she appears to have first discovered the breed in Italy when she traveled there in 1888. She obtained several such dogs in Florence, including Marco, with whom she achieved notable success at Crufts and elsewhere. Incidentally, Marco weighed 12 lb. A great lover of many different kinds of dogs, Queen Victoria owned a kennel of Pomeranians, bred under the prefix Windsor. Charles Henry Lane was invited to inspect Her Majesty's kennels and, as one might expect, he spoke highly of their circumstances, every care and consideration being shown for the dogs' happiness. He described the dogs primarily as what he termed "off-colors," although some were exceedingly pretty. Although some were larger, most were what he called "small-medium."

Some of these were exhibited at shows and there is rather an amusing of story of the time when Her Majesty wished to exhibit three Pomeranians of a color not usually shown in England. A special class was provided for her exhibits and two of them were lucky enough to be awarded joint first prize! So much did Queen Victoria love the breed that while

THE POMERANIAN IN ART

The British Museum houses an ancient Greek bronze jar from the second century B.C. On it is engraved a group of winged horses and at their feet is a small dog of Pomeranian type. On a famous street in Athens was a representation of a small spitz dog leaping up to the daughter of the family as she was taking her leave. The date of this is 56 B.C.

The famous artist Sir Thomas Gainsborough is one of several who often portrayed Pomeranians in his paintings. In London's Wallace Collection, there is a particularly famous painting of the actress Mrs. Robinson, who has a large white Pomeranian sitting by her side.

she was dying, her Pomeranian, Turi, was always on her bed. Aided in part by Queen Victoria's prominence, Britain's interest in the breed grew.

Mr. Gladstone was another prominent person who was much taken by the breed and is said to have owned a black Pomeranian. As the 20th century turned, there was a saying, "There's money in Poms," for they were selling for up to £250. Ounce for pound, Pomeranians were probably the most expensive breed of dog one could purchase. This said, supply soon overtook demand and the breed dropped rapidly in value. Pomeranians were bred from at a rapid rate, such as would certainly not be permitted by the English Kennel Club today.

A newspaper report gave an example of one bitch that whelped for the third time in May of 1903, when she was still under two years old. In her three litters, she had produced 24 puppies, all within the space of 54 weeks. Poor lady—it doesn't bear thinking about!

A great deal of inbreeding was going on at that time, and some signs of degeneration were evident, such as a tendency toward apple heads in smaller sized specimens. These smaller Poms possessed heads quite out of keeping with the fox-headed requirement of the breed.

A 1904 account states, "There is no species of ladies' pet-dog that has achieved such universal popularity in so short a time as the Pomeranian." Early in the century, several prominent people in dogs expressed their views on the breed. For Miss Hamilton, who regularly took top honors in the breed, her ideal Pomeranian was "a bright little creature, sparkling all over with life and fun, devoted to his master or mistress, and sharing all their joys

SHARING A CLASS IN THE UK

At Maidstone Show in 1882, Pomeranians and Maltese shared a class together. Then, at York and also at Henley-on-Thames the following year, Pomeranians and Poodles were exhibited alongside each other, a rather absurd arrangement! But to cap it all, at Hull in 1864, Pugs, King Charles or Blenheims and Pomeranians shared their class.

and sorrows as much as lies in a doggy's power." Miss Hamilton said she had come across many that had been almost human in their keenness of perception and expressed the utmost sympathy during times when their owners were distressed. She thought them as clever at tricks as Poodles but, though excitable by nature, they never allowed their anger to get the better of their discretion.

The Pomeranian Club drew up the first English breed standard in 1891, the year in which the club was founded. However, the larger specimens of the breed rather quickly fell out of fashion and, by the early years of the 20th century, breeders were already producing very small Pomeranians, more akin to the breed we recognize today.

In the beginning the breed was shown in two sizes, over and

Sir Thomas Gainsborough's portrait of the well-known actress, Mrs. Robinson, with her Pomeranian. Note how much larger the breed was in days gone by.

under 8 lb, but the larger size really failed to achieve a great deal of popularity. At Crufts in 1894, a resolution was passed that the weight of Pomeranians was to be divided thus: "Over and under 16 lb; over and under 7 lb. Those below 7 lb to be called Toys." Today in Britain, the size called for in the breed standard is only 1.8–2 kg (4–4.5 lb) for dogs and 2–2.5 kg (4.5–5.5 lb) for bitches. At most shows, however, division was mainly by color, a system that continued for some years, but as breeders discovered that small whites were difficult to breed, this color lost ground.

Entries at shows rose significantly from the breed's early years

This stuffed and mounted Pomeranian, presented to the British Museum of Natural History in 1930, was named Brownie.

Gainsborough's "Pomeranian and Puppy."

Ch. Eng. Boy Blue, winner of 15 champion prizes, circa 1906.

in the show ring. In 1890, not a single Pomeranian was shown, but there were 14 in 1891 and by 1901 the number had risen to 60. Frequently there were over 50 Pomeranian entries at a show, and sometimes a popular judge could command an entry of around 100, making 25 or so entries per class. In 1905, there were 105 Pomeranians entered at a show, confirming the breed's rapid rise in the popularity stakes.

In 1911, The Kennel Club attempted to stop trimming in all breeds, reasoning that dogs should be shown in a natural condition. As the Pomeranian is a trimmed breed, the coat appearing shaggy when the ears are covered with long hair, this caused uproar

Miss Alice
Horsfall and her
Poms, circa 1908.

Center spread:
This lovely
photograph
depicts a young
lady surrounded
by her white
Pomeranians,
circa 1919.

within breed circles and absurd
proposals were made to circum-
vent the issue. Thankfully the
situation did not last long, for in
April 1913, The Kennel Club
wrote to the Pomeranian Club
asking if it wished the Pomeranian to be scheduled among breeds
in which trimming was allowed.

Two years later, The Kennel
Club decided that all weights
were to be registered together and
that at Championship Shows only
one set of Challenge Certificates
(CCs) could be awarded. It had
been suggested that the heavier
dogs be registered as "Spitz." The
attempt to form a "Spitz" breed
failed even though some registrations were made at that time. Still,
in 1916, Certificates of Merit were
offered by the Pomeranian Club
for Pomeranians above 7 lb, an
idea that was discontinued
through lack of interest.

World War I caused great
disruption among the world of
dogs, and presumably because of
the breed's German connections,
the Pomeranian fell out of favor.
The breed had previously been
the top Toy breed, but this position was taken over by the

Champion Pomeranians owned by Mrs. Hall Walkers. From left to right: Eng. Ch. Dainty Boy, Eng. Ch. Gateacre Bibury Bell and Eng. Ch. Gateacre Dainty Belle. The painting was by famous dog artist Maud Earl, circa 1920. The apple in the foreground effectively gives size perspective to the dogs.

Miss Hamilton's famous kennel competed with Queen Victoria's and divided most of the honors with the Royal kennels. It was Miss Hamilton who won the first championship for a Pom.

Pekingese and later, in 1962, by the Yorkshire Terrier. By the 1930s, the size of Pomeranians had dropped markedly, down to 9 lb, and by then the coat had developed its characteristic deep frilling.

THE POMERANIAN IN AMERICA

In the US, the first Pomeranian to be recorded by the American Kennel Club (AKC) was Dick, who was registered in 1888. The breed was recognized in America in 1900. That same year, English judge, L. P. C. Astley awarded the first ever Best of Breed to a Pomeranian in this country. This was Mrs. Frank Smyth's Nubian Rebel, later to become a champion in the breed.

By 1909, the American Pomeranian Club had been accepted as a member club of the AKC and was designated as the parent club for the breed. Not too long after, it hosted the country's first Pomeranian specialty show at which another English judge, Mrs. L. C. Dyer, drew an entry of 138, finding her Best of Breed in the black Pomeranian, Ch. Canner Prince Charming.

The first regional Pomeranian specialty club was formed in the year 1912. This was the Western Pomeranian Club, formed in Chicago by Mrs. Hebden. Nine years later, in 1921, the American Pomeranian Club was incorporated.

During the 1930s, there was good attendance of Pomeranians at shows and a series of notable breeding lines were developed. By

From the 1920s, Sunfire of Dara, an orange Pom bred by Mrs. E. B. Goodall in 1928.

1958 the first official breed magazine was launched. This was *The Pomeranian Review*, whose first editor was James Arima.

The year 1961 was also a landmark in the history of the breed, for this was when the first American-bred bitch took Best in Show at an all-breed show. Bred by Mr. and Mrs. K. Terrel of Fort Worth, Texas, this clever bitch was Ch. Ridglea's Luscious Retta.

The years in which different colors within the breed have won high accolades are also interesting to note. It was in the early 1970s that Ch. Silva Lade's Gentle Ben was the first black Pomeranian to receive a Best in Show award, this at Penobscot Valley Kennel Club, but not until June 1981 was the first blue to be awarded the title of champion. This was Ch. Silva Lade's The Enforcer, bred, owned and handled by Dianne Johnson of Baltimore. Just four years later, her Ch. Silva Lade's

A spitz-like dog from an engraved bronze jar of Greek workmanship from the second century B.C. It is on display at the British Museum in London.

Webbun Fun and Webbun Frolic made their debut at the Crufts Dog Show in 1934 in the Litter Class for Poms. Both were awarded first prizes.

Almond Joy was the first chocolate and tan to take its championship title. However, the breed had to wait until 1996 for the very first brindle Pomeranian to be awarded the title of champion. This was Ch. Jan Le's Rumm Tumm Tigger, sired by Ch. Jan Le's Willie Makit and out of Jan Le's Quartrcup of Troubl, bred and owned by Judy Mahciz and Jane Lehtinen.

In recent decades, Pomeranians have gained both conformation championship titles as well as top awards at obedience trials. The first to gain dual titles was Ch. Nino of Thelcolynn UD, owned by Mrs. P. E. Lambert of Arlington. The title UD indicates that the dog has qualified at the highest level of obedience, Utility Dog.

In February 1988, a Pomeranian was awarded Best in Show at the Westminster Kennel Club Show in New York City's Madison Square Garden—another first for another Prince Charming! This was Olga Baker and Skip Piazza's Ch. Great Elms Prince Charming II ROMX, HOF, sired by Ch. Cedarwood's Image of Diamond and out of Great Elms Sweet Candy, ROMX. The judge on this great occasion was Michele Billings.

Pomeranians have also displayed their prowess in the field of good citizenship. The first Pom to achieve the Canine Good Citizen award was Margaret McKee's Ch Idlewyld Lavalier CDX, CGC, HOF, who was also the first dual-titled Pomeranian bred from dual-titled parents. In the agility world, 1995 was the year in which the first Pomeranian won a Novice Agility title, this being Kassel's Dandelion Down UD, NA (later OA), HOF, ROM. The following year, Ollie Blue Buster CDX, TD, OA, CGC, TT, GC was the clever Pomeranian that was the first to earn three performance titles.

> **"MAD DOG SCARE"**
> During a "mad dog scare" in New York, it was officially believed that Pomeranian-type dogs were responsible for the disease. In consequence, any dog vaguely resembling the breed was slaughtered. It is believed that the sharp-pointed muzzle may have been the reason behind this official decision regarding responsibility.

As years have gone by, Pomeranian registrations with the AKC have increased remarkably but, in the last few years, numbers have dropped slightly, though the breed is still in the top 10 or 15 in this country, registering between 25,000 to 30,000 or more!

While it is true that the early Pomeranians imported to the US from England were of the larger variety, today an average weight for a Pomeranian in America ranges between 3 and 8 lb. In the show ring, they tend to be between 4 and 6 lb. Some are even smaller, and are referred to as "Tiny" or "Teacup" size, though most breeders will not purposely breed to achieve such a

The famous Eng. Ch. Montacute Little Love, the puppy champion, was bred and shown by Mrs. Holroyd. The dog was a great winner in 1931, 1932 and 1933.

particularly small specimen of the breed. This is because extreme smallness brings with it severe veterinary problems, added to which the lifespan is usually shorter. Conversely, several poorly bred Pomeranians can far exceed the weight limit set down in the breed standard and can be as much as 10 or even 15 lb.

Surrounded by glory, Eng. Ch. Montacute Little Love, who miraculously became a champion while still a puppy, is shown among the trophies won in 1933.

CHARACTERISTICS OF THE

POMERANIAN

The Pomeranian is undoubtedly a breed with great appeal for those who want a small, compact, dainty dog with a happy, lively disposition, a big personality and a huge amount of energy. The breed's intelligence and incredible energy compensate for its diminutive size and, of course, the Pomeranian's dense double coat, found in a veritable array of colors, is the breed's crowning glory.

It is said that the Pomeranian is a dog that is made to be spoiled, and that both dog and owner are happiest when this is

At seven months of age, this Pom is developing his full adult plumage. Like all Poms, he appears alert and friendly.

so. Having said that, you should always be sensible about the way in which you spoil your Pom!

PHYSICAL CHARACTERISTICS

Today's Pomeranian is a tiny dog and, contrary to most larger breeds of dog, males are generally smaller than females, but even then the maximum weight called for in the breed standard is 7 lb. The Pomeranian is a soundly made, compact little dog that moves briskly, with something of a proud, strutting charm that gives the impression that he has a great big heart inside his tiny frame.

The Pomeranian's cute "foxy" head and charming expression are set off by tiny pricked ears. The profusely coated tail is carried well over the back, reaching to the head and helping to create the illusion of a circle.

COLOR AND COAT

The colors of the Pomeranian are many and varied, and the choice is enormous, with colors ranging from white through orange to black. Colors of nose pigment also alter according to coat color.

The profuse coat is a double one, with a soft, fluffy undercoat and straight, harsh-textured outer coat standing off from the body. Around the neck, on the chest and on the front of the shoulders, the coat is abundant and forms a frill. There is good feathering on the fore and hind legs, and the tail is covered with a profusion of long, harsh, spreading hair. This means that the coat does need attention, although grooming can undoubtedly be a pleasure for both dog and owner.

PERSONALITY

A dog with an incredible amount of energy, the Pomeranian is extroverted, lively and intelligent, and makes a delightful family member. It must never be forgotten that the Pomeranian is a member of the spitz family and can therefore be very loyal and protective of its owners. However, the Pomeranian can be rather reserved with strangers and does have a tendency to bark at them.

DOGS, DOGS, GOOD FOR YOUR HEART!

People usually purchase dogs for companionship, but studies show that dogs can help to improve their owners' health and level of activity, as well as lower a human's risk of coronary heart disease. Without even realizing it, when a person puts time into exercising, grooming and feeding a dog, he also puts more time into his own personal health care. Dog owners establish more routine schedules for their dogs to follow, which can have positive effects on their own health. Dogs also teach us patience, offer unconditional love and provide the joy of having a furry friend to pet!

The Pom's profuse outer coat is harsh-textured and protects the body. Owners must be prepared to devote time to the upkeep of this beautiful coat.

Well-behaved children make good friends for the Pomeranian. This Pom is enjoying a budding show career with his young mistress.

This is an alert and curious dog, always busy, but the Pomeranian can also be both bold and willful. As one of the more independent of the Toy breeds, the Pomeranian can be slightly sharp-tempered, but his affectionate nature is very endearing. Although of small stature, this breed has a resonant bark and makes a good watchdog.

It is necessary for a Pomeranian to know exactly who is boss, and he requires gentleness coupled with firmness in training. Otherwise, he may become overly demanding if allowed to get too much of his own way.

Although the Pomeranian is small enough to live in an apartment, townhouse or other home of limited size, and is a breed that will, to a large extent, exercise itself, owners should still provide their dogs with exercise on a regular basis. The Pomeranian can make an especially loyal companion for the elderly and can provide many happy years of pleasure and companionship.

TRAINABILITY
Because the Pomeranian is a quick learner and is intelligent as well, the breed seems always eager to learn. Obedience training seems to give Pomeranians great pleasure and this breed is highly likely to enjoy learning the odd trick or two. Although the Pomeranian is tiny compared with most other breeds, some do take part in agility trials, apparently with success!

POMERANIANS WITH CHILDREN
Because Pomeranians are so tiny, this breed is not generally recommended for families with small children. The danger is that children will treat the Pomeranian as a toy and might unintentionally do the dog harm. However, there are exceptions to any rule and a great deal depends upon the control and attitude of parents, as well as the sensitivity and intelligence of the children in question.

If Pomeranians are introduced to a family with young, active children, it is absolutely essential that parents have trained their children to treat

The Pomeranian must be trained with gentle firmness so he understands the rules of the household. A well-cared-for and trained Pom is a delightful companion to behold.

Poms get along well with other pets if properly socialized.

dogs gently, being neither rough nor aggressive. It must also be understood that young children should always be supervised when in the company of dogs in order that accidents do not happen.

WITH OTHER FAMILY PETS
When one animal is introduced to another, careful supervision is always essential. Many Pomeranians are quite prepared to associate with other animals that share the same house, but a lot depends on the personality of the other animal. An older dog or cat may not take readily to a newcomer to the household, although others might accept them easily. When a Pomeranian does find another canine or feline friend, usually the relationship is lasting and sincere.

Poms are small and delicate and should only be exposed to children who are properly instructed in how to handle them.

The Pomeranian can show aggression toward animals he doesn't know and is often all too ready to chase strange cats. Rarely is a Pomeranian afraid of other dogs, however large, so you should always be on the alert so that such a tiny dog comes to no harm when displaying his boldness!

HEALTH CONSIDERATIONS
Despite his small size, the Pomeranian is generally a healthy little dog, but, as in so many other breeds, certain

health problems arise. It is in the best interests of the breed for new owners to know what to look out for. If owners are aware of the problems that can occur, they are undoubtedly in an advantaged position to deal with them in the best manner possible. Some problems are genetic and are carried via heredity, while others are not.

LEG PROBLEMS

Pomeranians are known to suffer from trouble with the knee joints, known as patellar luxation, a problem that is fairly common among Toy breeds. Many dogs with patellar luxation live with the problem without experiencing pain, in part because the breed is so light in

THE JOYS OF YOGURT
At the first sign of any minor infection, the author has often found that live yogurt, administered orally, is of great benefit. This sometimes has the effect of rectifying the problem almost immediately, before a course of antibiotics becomes necessary.

weight. However, surgery has to be resorted to in severe cases. It is sensible to train your Pomeranian not to do any strenuous jumping, especially off high places, for this can result in damage to the knees. Climbing up and down stairs should also be restricted or, at the least, supervised. Another important factor is that a dog should not be overweight, as this is likely to exacerbate the problem.

DISC PROBLEMS

Occasionally Pomeranians can suffer from disc problems, and these can be very painful. The majority of vets treats this condition with steroids and restricted activity, usually with the dog's being confined to a crate for a couple of weeks. Disc problems should always be treated seriously and veterinary attention is essential at an early stage. Pomeranians are resilient dogs and some heal well enough to continue to enjoy active lives when they have fully recovered.

Poms love to play and require exercise to stay fit. Well-behaved children can be ideal playmates for Poms.

Begin taking care of your Pom's teeth at an early age. Active dental hygiene promises that your Pom will keep his teeth for a long time.

EYE PROBLEMS

Pomeranians can fairly frequently suffer eye infections, in part because their eyes are more exposed to dirt, dust and injury than the eyes of many other breeds. Always be sure to keep a careful check on the cleanliness and condition of your Pomeranian's eyes and, at the first sign of injury, especially if the eye is starting to turn blue in color, urgent veterinary attention is required. Early diagnosis and treatment can often save a dog's sight. Another problem within the breed can be excessive tearing, known as epiphora.

TEETH AND GUM PROBLEMS

As with many of the other smaller breeds, some Pomeranians lose their teeth at a relatively early age. It is therefore important to pay close attention to the care of teeth and gums so that they remain as healthy as possible, thereby preventing decay, infection and resultant loss.

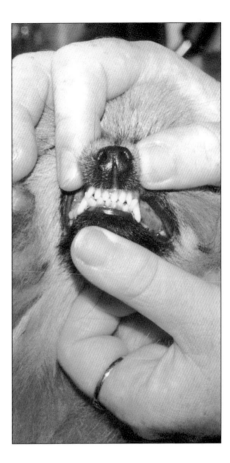

WEIGHTY CONCERNS

Elderly Pomeranians, like other dogs, can sometimes be prone to putting on excess weight. The profuse coat deceives an owner into thinking that the dog is of correct weight, when in fact it is too fat. Over-eating or feeding the wrong foods may be the cause. Often an older dog requires a slightly different diet from a younger one.

Infection in the gums may not just stop there. The bacteria from this type of infection is carried through the bloodstream, the result of which can be diseases of the liver, kidney, heart and joints. This is all the more reason to realize that efficient dental care is of utmost importance throughout a dog's life.

Feeding dry foods is recommended by many vets as a means of helping to keep teeth clean and in good condition, but of course regular, careful brushing with a veterinary toothpaste helps enormously.

Another dental problem that can occur in Pomeranians is retained deciduous teeth, meaning that a puppy's baby teeth may not drop out on their own. Should they still be in place when the adult teeth have begun to erupt, it is worth taking your puppy to the vet to see if they need extraction. If they remain in place when the new teeth have come through, they will push the adult teeth out of alignment.

OPEN FONTANEL

An open fontanel, also called a molera, is a hole in the skull, and this can sometimes be found in small Pomeranians. If sections of skull bone are actually floating, there can be serious problems, but otherwise this need not be a major worry. Obviously there is danger if the dog knocks his skull on the soft spot, but the coverings of the brain are tough and there is a fluid "cushion" that protects the brain from minor bumps.

Most open fontanels close by the time a Pomeranian is around one year old, but sometimes the center one does not close completely. Even in the latter case, many dogs so affected live long lives.

BREATHING DIFFICULTIES

Breathing difficulties in the Pomeranian can be caused by tracheal collapse. Many Pomeranians are prone to "gagging," but this should be monitored in case the problem is something more serious, in which case surgery may be needed. Some vets, however, make every effort to deal with the problem without surgery, and instead look more closely into conditions at home.

Some Pomeranians can suffer badly in smoky or dusty conditions, this being due to their tiny throats. Keeping them away from such environments can help greatly. Sometimes such an

SKIN PROBLEMS

Some Pomeranians suffer from skin problems, often termed "black skin disease." However, the cause must be investigated, for alopecia can be caused by many things, including hypothyroidism, Cushing's disease, Addison's disease, allergies, excessive female estrogen, stress, fleas, mites and mange.

In all, the Pomeranian is a healthy, long-lived companion that brings much joy to his lucky owners.

attack can also be brought on by over-excitement. On occasions when they do suffer a coughing attack, they should be picked up slowly and gently patted to reassure them.

HEART PROBLEMS
Occasionally Pomeranians, like many other breeds, suffer from heart problems. It is therefore sensible to request your vet to check your Pom's heart whenever you visit for routine examination or vaccination.

KIDNEY STONES
Kidney stones are not unknown in Pomeranians, but of course these can occur in many breeds and may appear in either sex. However, because the urethra of the male is longer and narrower than that of the female, obstruction is more common in males. Symptoms of kidney stones are frequent urination, bloody urine, dribbling urine, straining, weakness, depression, vomiting and pain, so it is evident that urgent veterinary advice should be sought. Although kidney stones can occur in dogs even less than two months old, they usually appear in adults between two and ten years of age.

WHELPING AND WHELPS
Newly born Pomeranian puppies are exceptionally tiny and can be held in the palm of your hand. Being so tiny and fragile, it is understandably important that they are treated with great care.

Although bitches are usually larger than males in this breed, small bitches can require Cesarean section. The likelihood of this should be discussed with your veterinarian prior to a mating taking place.

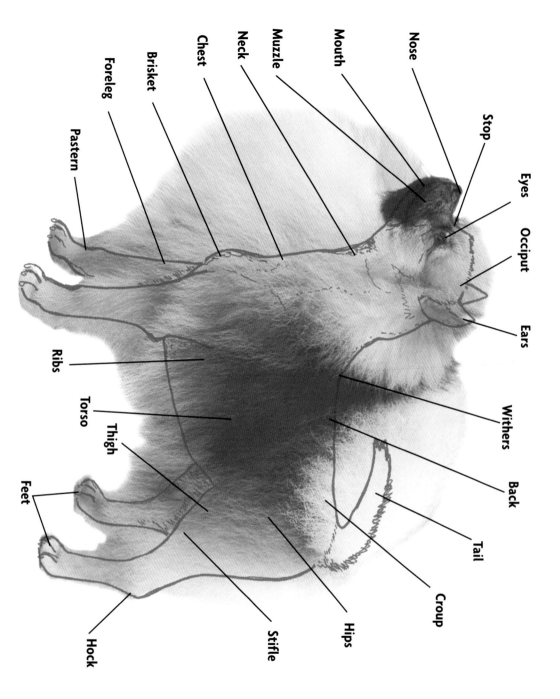

Nose

Stop

Eyes

Occiput

Ears

Withers

Back

Tail

Croup

Hips

Stifle

Hock

Feet

Torso

Thigh

Ribs

Pastern

Foreleg

Brisket

Chest

Neck

Muzzle

Mouth

Physical Structure of the Pomeranian

The American Kennel Club breed standard for the Pomeranian is effectively a "blue-print" for the breed. It sets down the various points of the dog in words, enabling a visual picture to be conjured up in the mind of the reader. However, this is more easily said than done. Not only do standards vary from country to country, but people's interpretations of breed standards vary also. It is this difference of interpretation that makes judges select different dogs for top honors, for their opinions differ as to which dog most closely fits the breed standard. That is not to say that a good dog does not win regularly under different judges, nor that an inferior dog may rarely even be placed at a show, at least not among quality competition.

The breed standard given here is that authorized by the American Kennel Club. It is comprehensive, and so is reasonably self-explanatory. However, as with most breeds, there are variances between the standards used in the US and that in Britain, where the Pomeranian first emerged as a show dog.

Notably, the British standard allows less latitude in weight,

Compact and short-backed describe the desirable appearance of the Pomeranian.

reading, "Ideal weight: dogs: 1.8–2 kgs (4–4.5 lb); bitches: 2–2.5 kgs (4.5–5.5 lb)." Another interesting point in the American standard is the statement that the skull should be closed, clearly steering breeders away from producing Pomeranians with open fontanels, whereas such a statement is not incorporated in Britain.

THE AMERICAN KENNEL CLUB STANDARD FOR THE POMERANIAN

General Appearance: The Pomeranian is a compact, short-backed, active toy dog. He has a soft, dense undercoat with a profuse harsh-textured outer

coat. His heavily plumed tail is set high and lies flat on his back. He is alert in character, exhibits intelligence in expression, is buoyant in deportment, and is inquisitive by nature. The Pomeranian is cocky, commanding, and animated as he gaits. He is sound in composition and action.

Size, Proportion, Substance: The average weight of the Pomeranian is from 3 to 7 pounds, with the ideal weight for the show specimen being 4 to 6 pounds. Any dog over or under the limits is objectionable. However, overall quality is to be favored over size. The distance from the point of shoulder to the point of buttocks is slightly shorter than from the highest point of the withers to the ground. The distance from the brisket to the ground is half the height at the withers. He is medium-boned, and the length of his legs is in proportion to a well-balanced frame. When examined, he feels sturdy.

Head: The head is in balance with the body. The muzzle is rather short, straight, fine, free of lippiness and never snipey. His expression is alert and may be referred to as fox-like. The skull is closed. The top of the skull is slightly rounded, but not domed. When viewed from the front and side, one sees small ears which are mounted high and carried erect. To form a wedge, visualize a line from the tip of the nose ascending through the center of the eyes and the tip of the ears. The eyes are dark, bright, medium in size and almond-shaped. They are set well into the skull on either side of a well-

Head study showing correct "foxy" expression.   **Ears are too big, eyes are too light, muzzle too long.**

A Pomeranian of correct type, balance and structure finished off with a mature stand off coat.

pronounced stop. The pigmentation is black on the nose and eye rims except self-colored in brown, beaver, and blue dogs. The teeth meet in a scissors bite. One tooth out of alignment is acceptable. Major Faults: Round, domed skull; undershot mouth; overshot mouth.

Neck, Topline, Body: The neck is short with its base set well into the shoulders to allow the head to be carried high. The back is short with a level topline. The body is compact and well-ribbed with brisket reaching the elbow. The plumed tail is one of the

characteristics of the breed, and lies flat and straight on the back.

Forequarters: The Pomeranian has sufficient layback of shoulders to carry the neck and head proud and high. The shoulders and legs are moderately muscled. The length of the shoulder blade and upper arm are equal. The forelegs are straight and parallel to each other. Height from elbows to withers approximately equals height from ground to elbow. The pasterns are straight and strong. The feet are well-arched, compact, and turn neither in nor out. He stands well up on his

toes. Dewclaws may be removed.
Major Faults: Down in pasterns.

Hindquarters: The angulation of
the hindquarters balances that of
the forequarters. The buttocks are
well behind the set of the tail.
The thighs are moderately
muscled with stifles that are
moderately bent and clearly
defined. The hocks are perpen-
dicular to the ground and the
legs are straight and parallel to
each other. The feet are well-
arched, compact, and turn
neither in nor out. He stands well
up on his toes. Dewclaws, if any,
on the hind legs may be
removed. Major Faults: Cow-
hocks or lack of soundness in
hind legs or stifles.

Gait: The Pomeranian's gait is
smooth, free, balanced and vigor-
ous. He has good reach in his
forequarters and strong drive
with his hindquarters. Each rear
leg moves in line with the foreleg
on the same side. To achieve
balance, his legs converge
slightly inward toward a center
line beneath his body. The rear
and front legs are thrown neither
in nor out. The topline remains
level, and his overall balance and
outline are maintained.

Coat: A Pomeranian is noted for
his double coat. The undercoat is
soft and dense. The outer coat is
long, straight, glistening and

FAULTS AT A GLANCE

Long backed, low
tail set, weak
pinched front and
matching weak
narrow rear,
upright shoulders,
ears large and too
wide set.

High on leg, weak
pasterns, cow-
hocked, flat feet.

Long backed,
low on leg,
"dwarfism."

This color is often called cream.

MEETING THE IDEAL

The American Kennel Club (AKC) defines a standard as: "A description of the ideal dog of each recognized breed, to serve as an ideal against which dogs are judged at shows." This "blueprint" is drawn up by the breed's recognized parent club, approved by a majority of its membership and then submitted to the AKC for approval. This is a complete departure from the way standards are handled in England, where all standards and changes are controlled by The Kennel Club.

The AKC states that "An understanding of any breed must begin with its standard. This applies to all dogs, not just those intended for showing." The picture that the standard draws of the dog's type, gait, temperament and structure is the guiding image used by breeders as they plan their programs.

harsh in texture. A thick undercoat will hold up and permit the guard hair to stand off from the Pomeranian's body. The coat is abundant from the neck and fore part of shoulders and chest, forming a frill which extends over the shoulders and chest. The head and leg coat is tightly packed and shorter in length than that of the body. The forequarters are well-feathered to the hock. The tail is profusely covered with long, harsh, spreading straight hair. Trimming for neatness and a clean outline is permissible. Major Faults: Soft, flat or open coat.

One of the most alluring qualities of the breed is its rainbow of coat colors.

Color: All colors, patterns, and variations there-of are allowed and must be judged on an equal basis. Patterns: Black and Tan— tan or rust sharply defined, appearing above each eye and on muzzle, throat, and forechest, on all legs and feet and below the tail. The richer the tan the more desirable; Brindle—the base color is gold, red, or orange-brindled with strong black cross stripes; Parti-color—is white with any other color distributed in patches with a white blaze preferred on

the head. Classifications: The Open Classes at specialty shows may be divided by color as follows: Open Red, Orange, Cream, and Sable; Open Black, Brown, and Blue; Open Any Other Color, Pattern, or Variation.

Temperament: The Pomeranian is an extrovert, exhibiting great intelligence and a vivacious spirit, making him a great companion dog as well as a competitive show dog. Even though a toy dog, the Pomeranian must be subject to the same requirements of soundness and structure prescribed for all breeds, and any deviation from the ideal described in the standard should be penalized to the extent of the deviation.

A NOTE ON THE STANDARD
Although a great deal can be learned from the breed standard, only by seeing good-quality, typical specimens can you really learn to appreciate the breed's merits. Therefore, readers interested in showing their Pomeranians should watch other dogs being exhibited, and learn as much as possible from established breeders and exhibitors.

This color is called black even though it has a red sheen.

This color is called by different names in different countries, including, but not limited to, red and orange.

EXPENSE OF BREEDING
The decision to breed your dog is one that must be considered carefully and researched thoroughly before moving into action. Some people believe that breeding will make their bitch happier or that it is an easy way to make money. Unfortunately, indiscriminate breeding only worsens the rampant problem of pet overpopulation, as well as putting a considerable dent in your pocketbook. As for the bitch, the entire process from mating through whelping is not an easy one and puts your pet under considerable stress. Last, but not least, consider whether or not you have the means to care for an entire litter of pups. Without a reputation in the field, your attempts to sell the pups may be unsuccessful.

BREEDER'S BLUEPRINT

If you are considering breeding your bitch, it is very important that you are familiar with the breed standard. Reputable breeders breed with the intention of producing dogs that are as close as possible to the standard and that contribute to the advancement of the breed. Study the standard for both physical appearance and temperament, and make certain your bitch and your chosen stud dog measure up.

It is sensible to attend judges' and breed seminars, often hosted by breed clubs. Here the finer points of the breed can be explained fully and discussed. There is usually a dog, or perhaps several, available for demonstration purposes, and there may even be an opportunity for participants to feel beneath the coat for the structure of the animal. Just a few elaborations on the breed standard are, however, worthy of brief comment here.

The late Harry Glover, a highly respected UK judge, described the breed as "a front-emphasis dog." By this, he meant that this was a dog with small hindquarters and a large, luxurious ruff around the neck, making it possible for a Pom to be held in the curve of an elbow. Though not specifically relating to the standard, this is an apt description and indeed the Pomeranian does lend itself to being carried over the arm in a highly individual way!

The straight, harsh-textured coat is wonderfully abundant around the neck, on the chest and on the forepart of the shoulders, with the frill extending over the shoulders, making a very pretty picture. It is not difficult to see why so many are attracted by the breed, even though they may not own a Pom.

But there is very much more to a Pomeranian than his coat. Beneath that coat should be a tiny dog that is soundly constructed in every department. A Pomeranian has to breathe, move and perform all his bodily functions like any other dog, so it is absolutely essential that the structure is sound throughout. The Pomeranian has been bred down in size over the years but, in doing so, soundness of overall construction should not have been lost, for that would indeed have been to the detriment of the breed.

The Pomeranian is a thoroughly attractive and active little breed, full of personality and vivacity. Thankfully, dedicated breeders have allowed the breed to develop into the wonderful little dog he is today, and it behooves all breeders to help him stay that way.

POMERANIAN

You have probably decided on a Pomeranian as your choice of pet following a visit to the home of a friend or acquaintance, where you have seen a sprightly Pom bouncing happily around the house, looking like a tiny ball of fun. However, as a potential owner, you must realize that a good deal of care, commitment and careful training goes into raising a boisterous puppy so that your pet turns into a well-behaved adult.

In deciding to take on a new puppy, you are committing yourself to many years of responsibility. No dog should be discarded after a few months, or even a few years, after the novelty has worn off. Instead, your Pomeranian should be joining your household to spend the rest of his days with you, so you should bear in mind that a healthy Pom can live well into his mid-teens.

Pomeranians should not be allowed to get too much of their own way, and although they are quick and eager learners, you will still need to carry out a certain amount of serious train-

"YOU BETTER SHOP AROUND!"

Finding a reputable breeder who sells healthy pups is very important, but make sure that the breeder you choose is not only someone you respect but also someone with whom you feel comfortable. Your breeder will be a resource long after you buy your puppy, and you must be able to call with reasonable questions without being made to feel like a pest! If you don't connect on a personal level, investigate some other breeders before making a final decision.

ARE YOU PREPARED?

Unfortunately, when a puppy is bought by someone who does not take into consideration the time and attention that dog ownership requires, it is the puppy who suffers when he is either abandoned or placed in a shelter by a frustrated owner. So all of the "homework" you do in preparation for your pup's arrival will benefit you both. The more informed you are, the more you will know what to expect and the better equipped you will be to handle the ups and downs of raising a puppy. Hopefully, everyone in the household is willing to do his part in raising and caring for the pup. The anticipation of owning a dog often brings a lot of promises from excited family members: "I will walk him every day," "I will feed him," "I will house-train him," etc., but these things take time and effort, and promises can easily be forgotten once the novelty of the new pet has worn off.

ing. You will need to take a firm but gentle approach in order to get the very best out of your pet, which is a representative of a strong-willed breed. Because of this, you must make it eminently clear from the very beginning that your dog is to do as you command.

Regarding cleanliness around the home, you will need to teach your puppy what is and is not expected. You will need to be consistent in your instructions; it is no good accepting certain behavior one day and not the next. Not only will your puppy simply not understand, he will be utterly confused. Your Pom will want to please you, so you will need to demonstrate clearly how your puppy is to achieve this.

Although the dog you are bringing into your home will be tiny, and therefore probably less troublesome in many ways than a large dog, there will undoubtedly be a period of settling in. This will be great fun, but you must be prepared for mishaps around the home during the first few weeks of your life together. It will be important that precious ornaments are kept well out of harm's way, and you will have to think twice about where you place hot cups of coffee or anything breakable. Accidents can and do happen, so you will need to

This young Pom is barely a handful, but you will soon realize that any dog can be a real "handful" if not properly trained.

The Pom puppy you select should not appear timid or fearful, though being such a small puppy can be more overwhelming than a human can imagine.

think ahead so as to avoid these. Electric cables must be carefully concealed, and your puppy must be taught where and where not to go.

Before making your commitment to a new puppy, do also think carefully about your future vacation plans. If you have thought things through carefully and discussed the matter thoroughly with all members of your family, hopefully you will have come to the right decision. If you decide that a Pomeranian should join your family, this will hopefully be a happy, long-term relationship for all parties concerned.

BUYING A POMERANIAN PUPPY

Although you may be looking for a Pomeranian as a pet, rather than as a show dog, this does not mean that you want a dog that is in any way "second-rate." A caring breeder will have brought up the entire litter of puppies with the same amount of dedication, and a puppy destined for a pet home should be just as healthy and outgoing as one that will end up in the show ring.

Because you have carefully selected this breed, you will want a Pom that is a typical specimen, both in looks and in temperament. In your endeavors to find such a puppy, you will have to select the breeder with care. The American Kennel Club will be able to give you names of contacts within Pomeranian or toy breed clubs. These people can possibly put you in touch with breeders who

DOING YOUR HOMEWORK
In order to know whether or not a puppy will fit into your lifestyle, you need to assess his personality. A good way to do this is to interact with his parents. Your pup inherits not only his appearance but also his personality and temperament from the sire and dam. If the parents are fearful or overly aggressive, these same traits may likely show up in your puppy.

may have puppies for sale. However, although they can point you in the right direction, it will be up to you to do your homework carefully.

Even though you are probably not looking for a show dog, it is always a good idea to visit a show so that you can see quality specimens of the breed. This will also give you an opportunity to meet breeders who will probably be able to answer some of your queries. In addition, you will get some idea about which breeders appear to take most care of their stock, and which are likely to have given their puppies the best possible start in life.

When buying your puppy, you will need to know about vaccinations, those already given and those still due. It is important that any injections already given by a veterinarian have documentary evidence to prove this. A worming routine is also vital for any young puppy, so the breeder should be able to tell you exactly what treatment has been given, when it has been administered and how you should continue.

Clearly, when selecting a puppy, the one you choose must be in good condition. The coat should look healthy and there should be no discharge from eyes or nose. Ears should also be clean, and of course there

TEMPERAMENT COUNTS

Your selection of a good puppy can be determined by your needs. A show potential or a good pet? It is your choice. Every puppy, however, should be of good temperament. Although show-quality puppies are bred and raised with emphasis on physical conformation, responsible breeders strive for equally good temperament. Do not buy from a breeder who concentrates solely on physical beauty at the expense of personality.

should be absolutely no sign of parasites. Check that there is no rash on the skin, and the puppy you choose should not have evidence of diarrhea.

Finally, a few words of advice. You must buy your puppy from a reputable source—a breeder—and the breeder you select must be responsible and ethical. Members of breed clubs must follow strict codes of ethics in their breeding programs. Those who don't are only to the detriment of the breed.

Always insist that you see the puppy's dam and, if possible, the sire. Frequently the sire will not be owned by the breeder of the litter, but a photograph should be available for you to see. Ask if the breeder has any other of the puppy's relations that you could meet. For example, there may be an older half-sister or half-brother and it would be interesting to see how they have turned out, their eventual size, coat quality, temperament and so on.

Be sure, too, that if you decide to buy a puppy, all relevant documentation is provided at the time of sale. You will need a copy of the pedigree, registration documents, sales agreement, vaccination certificates and a feeding chart so that you know exactly how the puppy has been fed and how you should continue. Some breeders provide their puppy buyers with a small amount of food. This prevents the risk of an upset tummy, allowing for a gradual change of diet if that particular brand of food is not readily available.

The gender of your puppy is largely a matter of personal taste. The difference in size is somewhat noticeable, with bitches slightly larger than dogs. Coloration should not be too much of a concern with this breed, which is available in a variety of colors. Because litters are small, your choice may be somewhat limited.

Breeders commonly allow visitors to see the litter by around the fifth or sixth week, and puppies leave for their new homes around the tenth or twelfth week. Breeders who permit their puppies to leave early are more interested in

PUPPY PERSONALITY

When a litter becomes available to you, choosing a pup out of all those adorable faces will not be an easy task! Sound temperament is of utmost importance, but each pup has its own personality and some may be better suited to you than others. A feisty, independent pup will do well in a home with older children and adults, while quiet, shy puppies will thrive in a home with minimal noise and distractions. Your breeder knows the pups best and should be able to guide you in the right direction.

your money than their puppies' well-being. Puppies need to learn the rules of the trade from their dams, and most dams continue teaching the pups manners and dos and don'ts during their time at the breeder's. Breeders spend significant amounts of time with the Pomeranian toddlers so that they are able to interact with the "other species," i.e., humans. Given the long history that dogs and humans have, bonding between the two species is natural but must be nurtured. A well-bred, well-socialized Pomeranian pup wants nothing more than to be near you and please you.

Always check the bite of your selected puppy to be sure that it is neither overshot or undershot. This may not be too noticeable on a young puppy, but it is important to check the bite for soundness.

COMMITMENT OF OWNERSHIP

After considering all of these factors, you have most likely already made some very important decisions about selecting your puppy. You have chosen a Pomeranian, which means that you have decided which characteristics you want in a dog and what type of dog will best fit into your family and lifestyle. If you have selected a breeder,

PUPPY APPEARANCE
Your puppy should have a well-fed appearance but not a distended abdomen, which may indicate worms or incorrect feeding, or both. The body should be firm, with a solid feel. The skin of the abdomen should be pale pink and clean, without signs of scratching or rash. Both front and hind dewclaws may be removed; check to see if the breeder has had this done.

you have gone a step further—you have done your research and found a responsible, conscientious person who breeds quality Pomeranians and who should be a reliable source of help as you and your puppy adjust to life together. If you have observed a litter in action, you have obtained a firsthand look at the dynamics of a puppy "pack" and, thus, you should learn about each pup's individual personality—perhaps you have even found one that particularly appeals to you.

However, even if you have not yet found the Pomeranian puppy of your dreams, observing pups will help you learn to recognize certain behaviors and to determine what a pup's behavior indicates about his temperament. You will be able to pick out which pups are the leaders, which ones are less outgoing, which ones are confident, which ones are shy, playful, friendly, aggressive, etc. Equally as important, you will learn to recognize what a healthy pup should look and act like. All of these things will help you in your search, and when you find the Pomeranian that was meant for you, you will know it!

Researching your breed, selecting a responsible breeder and observing as many pups as possible are all important steps on the way to dog ownership. It may seem like a lot of effort... and you have not even brought the pup home yet! Remember, though, you cannot be too careful when it comes to deciding on the type of dog you want and finding out about your prospective pup's background. Buying a puppy is not—or *should* not

PEDIGREE VS. REGISTRATION CERTIFICATE

Too often new owners are confused between these two important documents. Your puppy's pedigree, essentially a family tree, is a written record of a dog's genealogy of three generations or more. The pedigree will show you the names as well as performance titles of all the dogs in your pup's background. Your breeder must provide you with a registration application, with his part properly filled out. You must complete the application and send it to the AKC with the proper fee. Every puppy must come from a litter that has been AKC-registered by the breeder, born in the US and from a sire and dam that are also registered with the AKC.

The seller must provide you with complete records to identify the puppy. The AKC requires that the seller provide the buyer with the following: breed; sex, color and markings; date of birth; litter number (when available); names and registration numbers of the parents; breeder's name; and date sold or delivered.

PET INSURANCE

Just like you can insure your car, your house and your own health, you likewise can insure your dog's health. Investigate a pet insurance policy by talking to your vet. Depending on the age of your dog, the breed and the kind of coverage you desire, your policy can be very affordable. Most policies cover accidental injuries, poisoning and thousands of medical problems and illnesses, including cancers. Some carriers also offer routine care and immunization coverage.

be—just another whimsical purchase. This is one instance in which you actually do get to choose your own family! You may be thinking that buying a puppy should be fun—it should not be so serious and so much work. Keep in mind that your puppy is not a cuddly stuffed toy or decorative ornament, but a creature that will become a real member of your family. You will come to realize that, while buying a puppy is a pleasurable and exciting endeavor, it is not something to be taken lightly. Relax...the fun will start when the pup comes home!

Always keep in mind that a puppy is nothing more than a baby in a furry disguise...a baby who is virtually helpless in a human world and who trusts his owner for fulfillment of his basic needs for survival. In addition to food, water and shelter, your pup needs care, protection, guidance and love.

Breeders rarely release Pomeranian puppies until they are close to three months old, given the breed's petite size and frailty.

Your Pom puppy will welcome a comfy dog bed and a safe, tasty chew toy.

If you are not prepared to commit to this, then you are not prepared to own a dog.

"Wait a minute," you say. "How hard could this be? All of my neighbors own dogs and they seem to be doing just fine. Why should I have to worry about all of this?" Well, you should not worry about it; in fact, you will probably find that once your Pomeranian pup gets used to his new home, he will fall into his place in the family quite naturally. But it never hurts to emphasize the commitment of dog ownership. With some time and patience, it is really not too difficult to raise a curious and exuberant Pomeranian pup to be a well-adjusted and well-mannered adult dog— a dog that could be your most loyal friend.

PREPARING PUPPY'S PLACE IN YOUR HOME

Researching your breed and finding a breeder are only two aspects of the "homework" you will have to do before bringing your Pomeranian puppy home. You will also have to prepare your home and family for the new addition. Much as you would prepare a nursery for a newborn baby, you will need to designate a place in your home that will be the puppy's own. How you prepare your home will depend on how much freedom the dog will be allowed. Whatever you decide, you must ensure that he has a place that he can "call his own."

When you bring your new puppy into your home, you are bringing him into what will become his home as well. Obviously, you did not buy a puppy so that he could run your

YOUR SCHEDULE . . .
If you lead an erratic, unpredictable life, with daily or weekly changes in your work requirements, consider the problems of owning a puppy. The new puppy has to be fed regularly, socialized (loved, petted, handled, introduced to other people) and, most importantly, allowed to go outdoors for house-training. As the dog gets older, he can be more tolerant of deviations in his feeding and relief schedule.

household, but in order for a puppy to grow into a stable, well-adjusted dog, he has to feel comfortable in his surroundings. Remember, he is leaving the warmth and security of his mother and littermates, as well as the familiarity of the only place he has ever known, so it is important to make his transition as easy as possible. By preparing a place in your home for the puppy, you are making him feel as welcome as possible in a strange new place. It should not take him long to get used to it, but the sudden shock of being transplanted is somewhat traumatic for a young pup. Imagine how a small child would feel in the same situation—that is how your puppy must be feeling. It is up to you to reassure him and to let him know, "Little fur ball, you are going to like it here!"

WHAT YOU SHOULD BUY

CRATE
To someone unfamiliar with the use of crates in dog training, it may seem like punishment to shut a dog in a crate, but this is not the case at all. Most breeders advocate crate training and recommend crates as preferred tools for show puppies as well as pet puppies. Crates are not cruel—crates have many humane and highly effective

QUALITY FOOD
All dogs need a good-quality food with an adequate supply of protein to develop their bones and muscles properly. Most dogs are not picky eaters but, unless fed properly, can quickly succumb to skin problems.

uses in dog care and training. For example, crate training is a very popular and very successful housebreaking method. A crate can keep your dog safe during travel and, perhaps most importantly, a crate provides your dog with a place of his own in your home. It serves as a "doggie bedroom" of sorts—your Pomeranian can curl up in his crate when he wants to sleep or when he just needs a break. Many dogs sleep in their crates overnight. With soft

PHOTO COURTESY OF DOSKOCIL.

to each type. For example, a wire crate is more open, allowing the air to flow through and affording the dog a view of what is going on around him, while a fiberglass crate is sturdier. Both can double as travel crates, providing protection for the dog in the car, though the fiberglass crate is used for air travel. The size of the crate is another thing to consider. With a small breed like the Pom, any small crate will be fine to accommodate your dog both as a pup and at full size.

BEDDING

A crate mat in the dog's crate will help the dog feel more at home and you may also like to add in a small blanket. This will take the place of the leaves, twigs, etc., that the pup would use in the wild to make a den; the pup can make his own "burrow" in the crate. Although your pup is far removed from his den-making ancestors, the denning instinct is still a part of his genetic makeup. Second, until you bring your pup home, he has been sleeping amid the warmth of his mother and littermates, and while a blanket is not the same as a warm, breathing body, it still provides heat and something with which to snuggle. You will want to wash your pup's bedding frequently in case he has an accident in

bedding and a favorite toy, a crate becomes a cozy pseudo-den for your dog. Like his ancestors, he too will seek out the comfort and retreat of a den—you just happen to be providing him with something a little more luxurious than what his early ancestors enjoyed.

As far as purchasing a crate, the type that you buy is up to you. It will most likely be one of the two most popular types: wire or fiberglass. There are advantages and disadvantages

his crate, and replace or remove any blanket or pad that becomes ragged and starts to fall apart.

Toys

Toys are a must for dogs of all ages, especially for curious, playful pups. Puppies are the "children" of the dog world, and what child does not love toys? Chew toys provide enjoyment to both dog and owner—your dog will enjoy playing with his favorite toys, while you will enjoy the fact that they distract him from your expensive shoes and leather sofa. Puppies love to chew; in fact, chewing is a physical need for pups as they are teething, and

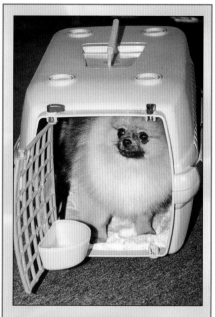

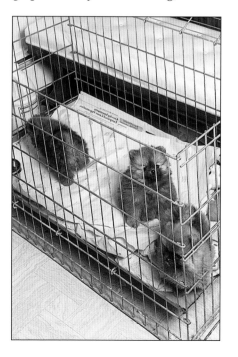

CRATE-TRAINING TIPS

During crate training, you should partition off the section of the crate in which the pup stays. If he is given too big an area, this will hinder your training efforts. Crate training is based on the fact that a dog does not like to soil his sleeping quarters, so it is ineffective to keep a pup in a crate that is so big that he can eliminate in one end and get far enough away from it to sleep. Also, you want to make the crate den-like for the pup. Blankets and a favorite toy will make the crate cozy for the small pup; as he grows, you may want to evict some of his "roommates" to make more room. It will take some coaxing at first, but be patient. Given some time to get used to it, your pup will adapt to his new home-within-a-home quite nicely.

Breeders often raise the litter on newspaper or similar material. Do not use newspaper to line your Pom's crate or it may encourage him to urinate there.

everything looks appetizing! The full range of your possessions—from an old tennis shoe to Oriental carpet—is fair game in the eyes of a teething pup. Puppies are not all that discerning when it comes to finding something to literally "sink their teeth into"—everything tastes great!

Breeders advise owners to resist stuffed toys, because they can become de-stuffed in no time. The overly excited pup may ingest the stuffing, which is neither digestible nor nutritious.

Similarly, squeaky toys are quite popular, but must be avoided for the Pomeranian.

Perhaps a squeaky toy can be used as an aid in training, but not for free play. If a pup "disembowels" one of these, the small plastic squeaker inside can be dangerous if swallowed. Monitor the condition of all your pup's toys carefully and get rid of any that have been chewed to the point of becoming potentially dangerous.

Be careful of natural bones, which have a tendency to splinter into sharp, dangerous pieces. Also be careful of rawhide, which can turn into pieces that are easy to swallow and become a mushy mess on your carpet.

You can cosset your Pom puppy as much as your purse will allow. This darling puppy is enjoying his luxurious new home with his very own furniture.

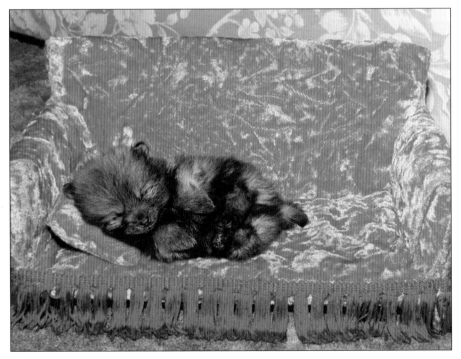

Leash

A nylon leash is probably the best option, as it is the most resistant to puppy teeth should your pup take a liking to chewing on his leash. Of course, this is a habit that should be nipped in the bud, but, if your pup likes to chew on his leash, he has a very slim chance of being able to chew through the strong nylon. Nylon leashes are also lightweight, which is good for a young Pomeranian who is just getting used to the idea of walking on a leash. For everyday walking and safety purposes, the nylon leash is a good choice. As your pup grows up and gets used to walking on the leash, you may want to purchase a flexible leash. These leashes allow you to extend the length to give the dog a broader area to explore or to shorten the length to keep the dog close to you.

Collar

Your pup should get used to wearing a collar all the time since you will want to attach his ID tags to it. Plus, you have to attach the leash to something! A lightweight nylon collar is a good choice; make sure that it fits snugly enough so that the pup cannot wriggle out of it, but is loose enough so that it will not be uncomfortably tight around the pup's

TOYS, TOYS, TOYS!

With a big variety of dog toys available, and so many that look like they would be a lot of fun for a dog, be careful in your selection. It is amazing what a set of puppy teeth can do to an innocent-looking toy; so, obviously, safety is a major consideration. Be sure to choose the most durable products that you can find. Hard nylon bones and toys are a safe bet, and many of them are offered in different scents and flavors that will be sure to capture your dog's attention. It is always fun to play a game of fetch with your dog, and there are balls and flying discs that are specially made to withstand dog teeth.

Your local pet shop will have many light leashes from which you can choose an appropriate leash for your Pom.

FINANCIAL RESPONSIBILITY

Grooming tools, collars, leashes, a crate, a dog bed and, of course, toys will be expenses to you when you first obtain your pup, and the cost will continue throughout your dog's lifetime. If your puppy damages or destroys your possessions (as most puppies surely will!) or something belonging to a neighbor, you can calculate additional expense. There is also flea and pest control, which every dog owner faces more than once. You must be able to handle the financial responsibility of owning a dog.

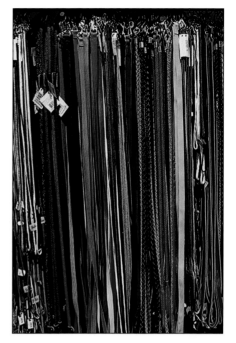

neck. You should be able to fit a finger between the pup and the collar. It may take some time for your pup to get used to wearing the collar, but soon he will not even notice that it is there.

FOOD AND WATER BOWLS

Your pup will need two bowls, one for food and one for water. You may want two sets of bowls, one for inside and one for outside, depending on where the dog will be fed and where he will be spending time. Stainless steel or sturdy plastic bowls are popular choices. Plastic bowls are more chewable. Dogs tend not to chew on the

Who can resist the smile of a Pom?

PHOTO COURTESY OF MIKKI PET PRODUCTS.

steel variety, which can be sterilized. It is important to buy sturdy bowls since anything is in danger of being chewed by puppy teeth and you do not want your dog to be constantly chewing apart his bowl (for his safety and for your wallet!).

CLEANING SUPPLIES

You will have to clean up after your puppy until you have completed house-training. Accidents will occur, which is okay in the beginning because the puppy does not know any better. All you can do is be prepared to clean up any accidents. Old rags, paper towels, newspapers and a safe disinfectant are good to have on hand.

BEYOND THE BASICS

The items previously discussed are the bare necessities. You will find out what else you need as you go along—grooming supplies, flea/tick protection, baby gates to partition a room, etc. These things will vary depending on your situation, but it is important that you have everything you need to feed and make your Pomeranian comfortable in his first few days at home.

PUPPY-PROOFING

Aside from making sure that your Pomeranian will be comfortable in your home, you also have to make sure that your home is safe for your Pomeranian. This means taking precautions that your pup will not get into anything he should not get into and that there is nothing within his reach that may harm him should he sniff it, chew it, inspect it, etc. This probably seems obvious since, while you are primarily concerned with your pup's safety, at the same time you do not want your belongings to be ruined. Breakables should be placed out of reach if your dog is to have full run of the house. If he is to be limited to certain places within the house, keep any potentially dangerous items in the "off-limits" areas. An

Your local pet shop usually has various devices to help make cleaning up after your dog easier.

Poms, like all dogs, love to chew. Use toys made especially for dogs because the dyes and materials used are dog-safe.

The inquisitive Pomeranian will want to explore every good-smelling corner of his new home. Be sure that all flowers and houseplants are non-toxic to dogs.

THE RIDE HOME

Taking your dog from the breeder to your home in a car can be a very uncomfortable experience for both of you. The puppy will have been taken from his warm, friendly, safe environment and brought into a strange new environment—an environment that moves! Be prepared for loose bowels, urination, crying, whining and even fear biting. With proper love and encouragement when you arrive home, the stress of the trip should quickly disappear.

electrical cord can pose a danger should the puppy decide to taste it—and who is going to convince a pup that it would not make a great chew toy? Cords should be fastened tightly against the wall. If your dog is going to spend time in a crate, make sure that there is nothing near his crate that he can reach if he sticks his curious little nose or paws through the openings. Keep all household cleaners and chemicals where the dog cannot get to them; antifreeze is especially dangerous.

It is also important to make sure that the outside of your home is safe. Of course your puppy should never be unsupervised, but a pup let loose in the yard will want to run and explore, and he should be granted that freedom. Do not let a fence give you a false sense of security; you would be surprised how crafty (and persistent) a dog can be in working out how to dig under

SKULL & CROSSBONES
Thoroughly puppy-proof your house before bringing your puppy home. Never use cockroach or rodent poisons or plant fertilizers in any area accessible to the puppy. Avoid the use of toilet cleaners. Most dogs are born with "toilet-bowl sonar" and will take a drink if the lid is left open. Also keep the trash secured and out of reach.

and squeeze his way through small holes, or to climb over a fence. The remedy is to make the fence high enough so that it really is impossible for your dog to get over it, and well embedded into the ground. Be sure to secure any gaps in the fence. Check the fence periodically to ensure that it is in good shape and make repairs as needed; a very determined pup may return to the same spot to

Your new Pom puppy will rely on you for his most important requirement: his safety.

For generations, Pomeranians have been affectionate and reliable companions for children and adults alike.

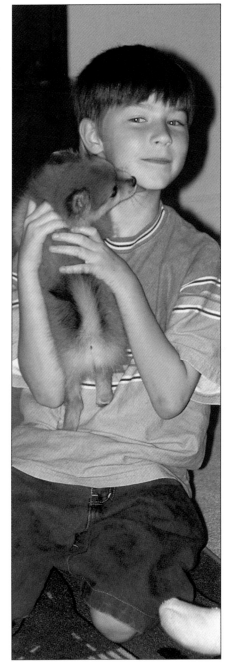

"work on it" until he is able to get through.

FIRST TRIP TO THE VET
You have picked out your puppy, and your home and family are ready. Now all you have to do is collect your Pomeranian from the breeder and the fun begins, right? Well...not so fast. Something else you need to prepare is your pup's first trip to the veterinarian. Perhaps the breeder can recommend someone in the area who specializes in Pomeranians, or maybe you know some other Pomeranian owners who can suggest a good vet. Either way, you should have an appointment arranged for your pup before you pick him up and plan on taking him for an exam-

HOW VACCINES WORK
If you've just bought a puppy, you surely know the importance of having your pup vaccinated, but do you understand how vaccines work? Vaccines contain the same bacteria or viruses that cause the disease you want to prevent, but they have been chemically modified so that they don't cause any harm. Instead, the vaccine causes your dog to produce antibodies that fight the harmful bacteria. Thus, if your dog is exposed to the disease in the future, the antibodies will destroy the viruses or bacteria.

ination before bringing him home or very soon after.

The pup's first visit will consist of an overall examination to make sure that the pup does not have any problems that are not apparent to you. The veterinarian will also set up a schedule for the pup's vaccinations; the breeder will inform you of which ones the pup has already received and the vet can continue from there.

INTRODUCTION TO THE FAMILY

Everyone in the house will be excited about the puppy's coming home and will want to pet him and play with him, but it is best to make the introductions low-key so as not to overwhelm the puppy. He is apprehensive already. It is the first time he has been separated from his mother and the breeder, and the ride to your home is likely to be the first time he has been in a car. The last thing you want to do is smother him, as this will only frighten him further. This is not to say that human contact is not extremely necessary at this stage, because this is the time when a connection between the pup and his human family is formed. Gentle petting and soothing words should help console him, as well as just putting him down and letting him explore on his

HOME WITH THE MANGE
Many young dogs suffer from demodectic mange, sometimes called red mange. All breeds of dog have suffered from demodectic mange, and any dog can be at risk. The mange manifests itself as localized infections on the face, muzzle, neck and limbs. The symptoms include hair loss and red, scaly skin. Vets routinely treat demodectic mange so that secondary infections are avoided. Many breeders remove known carriers from their programs.

own (under your watchful eye, of course).

The pup may approach the family members or may busy himself with exploring for a while. Gradually, each person should spend some time with the pup, one at a time, crouching down to get as close to the pup's level as possible and letting him sniff each person's hands and petting him gently. He definitely needs human attention and he needs to be touched—this is how to form an immediate bond. Just remember that the pup is experiencing a lot of things for the first time, at the same time. There are new people, new noises, new smells and new things to investigate, so be gentle, be affectionate and be as comforting as you can be.

PUP MEETS WORLD

Thorough socialization includes not only meeting new people but also being introduced to new experiences such as riding in the car, having his coat brushed, hearing the television, walking in a crowd—the list is endless. The more your pup experiences, and the more positive the experiences are, the less of a shock and the less frightening it will be for your pup to encounter new things.

YOUR PUP'S FIRST NIGHT HOME

You have traveled home with your new charge safely in his crate or a friend's lap. He's been to the vet for a thorough check-up, he's been weighed, his papers examined; perhaps he's even been vaccinated and wormed as well. He's met the family and licked the whole family, including the excited children and the less-than-happy cat. He's explored his area, his new bed, the yard and anywhere else he's been permitted. He's eaten his first meal at home and relieved himself in the proper place. He's heard lots of new sounds, smelled new friends and seen more of the outside world than ever before.

That was just the first day! He's worn out and is ready for bed...or so you think!

It's puppy's first night and you are ready to say "Good night"—keep in mind that this is puppy's first night ever to be sleeping alone. His dam and littermates are no longer at paw's length and he's a bit scared, cold and lonely. Be reassuring to your new family member, but this is not the time to spoil him and give in to his inevitable whining.

Puppies whine. They whine to let others know where they are and hopefully to get company out of it. Place your pup in his new bed or crate in his room and close the crate door. Mercifully, he may fall asleep without a peep. When the inevitable occurs, ignore the whining: he is fine. Be strong and keep his interests in mind. Do not allow your heart to become guilty and visit the pup. He will fall asleep.

Many breeders recommend placing a piece of bedding from his former home in his new bed so that he recognizes the scent of his littermates. Others still advise placing a hot water bottle in his bed for warmth. This latter may be a good idea provided the pup doesn't attempt to suckle—he'll get good and wet and may not fall asleep so fast.

Puppy's first night can be somewhat stressful for the pup and his new family. Remember

It may take a little while for your new Pomeranian puppy to adjust to his new home. Don't rush things—your pup will feel comfortable quite soon.

that you are setting the tone of nighttime at your house. Unless you want to play with your pup every night at 10 p.m., midnight and 2 a.m., don't initiate the habit. Your family will thank you, and so will your pup!

TRAINING TIP

Training your puppy takes much patience and can be frustrating at times, but you should see results from your efforts. If you have a puppy that seems untrainable, take him to a trainer or behaviorist. The dog may have a personality problem that requires the help of a professional, or perhaps you need help in learning how to train your dog.

PREVENTING PUPPY PROBLEMS

SOCIALIZATION

Now that you have done all of the preparatory work and have helped your pup get accustomed to his new home and family, it is about time for you to have some fun! Socializing your Pomeranian pup gives you the opportunity to show off your new friend, and your pup gets to reap the benefits of being an adorable furry creature that people will want to pet and, in general, think is absolutely precious!

Besides getting to know his new family, your puppy should

be exposed to other people, animals and situations, but of course he must not come into close contact with dogs you don't know well until his course of injections is fully complete. Socialization will help your pup become well adjusted as he grows up and less prone to being timid or fearful of the new things he will encounter. Your pup's socialization began at the breeder's but now it is your responsibility to continue it. The socialization he receives up until the age of 12 weeks is the most critical, as this is the time when he forms his impressions of the outside world. The breeder is especially careful during the eight-to-ten-week period, also known as the fear period. The interaction he receives during this time should be gentle and reassuring. Lack of socialization can manifest itself in fear and aggression as the dog grows up. He needs lots of human contact, affection, handling and exposure to other animals.

DON'T EAT THE DAISIES!

Many plants and flowers are beautiful to look at, but can be highly toxic if ingested by your dog. Reactions range from abdominal pain and vomiting to convulsions and death. If the following plants are in your home, remove them. If they are outside your house or in your garden, avoid accidents by making sure your dog is never left unsupervised in those locations.

Azalea
Belladonna
Bird of Paradise
Bulbs
Calla lily
Cardinal flower
Castor bean
Chinaberry tree
Daphne

Dumb cane
Dutchman's breeches
Elephant's ear
Hydrangea
Jack-in-the-pulpit
Jasmine
Jimsonweed
Larkspur
Laurel
Lily of the valley

Mescal bean
Mushrooms
Nightshade
Philodendron
Poinsettia
Prunus species
Tobacco
Yellow jasmine
Yews, *Taxus* species

MANNERS MATTER

During the socialization process, a puppy should meet people, experience different environments and definitely be exposed to other canines. Through playing and interacting with other dogs, your puppy will learn lessons, ranging from controlling the pressure of his jaws by biting his littermates to the inner-workings of the canine pack that he will apply to his human relationships for the rest of his life. That is why removing a puppy from its litter too early can be detrimental to the pup's development.

Once your pup has received his necessary vaccinations, feel free to take him out and about (on his leash, of course). Walk him around the neighborhood, take him on your daily errands, let people pet him, let him meet other dogs and pets, etc. Puppies do not have to try to make friends; there will be no shortage of people who will want to introduce themselves. Just make sure that you carefully supervise each meeting. If the neighborhood children want to say hello, for example, that is great—children and pups most often make great companions. However, sometimes an excited child can unintentionally handle a pup too roughly, or an overzealous pup can playfully nip a little too hard. You want

to make socialization experiences positive ones. What a pup learns during this very formative stage will impact his attitude toward future encounters. You want your dog to be comfortable around everyone. A pup that has a bad experience with a child may grow up to be a dog that is shy around or aggressive toward children.

Making friends is one of the Pomeranian puppy's God-given gifts!

A puppy's first encounter with a child or another pet in the home must be carefully supervised. A negative first meeting can hurt or emotionally scar a young pup.

CONSISTENCY IN TRAINING

Dogs, being pack animals, naturally need a leader, or else they try to establish dominance in their packs. When you bring a dog into your family, the choice of who becomes the leader and who becomes the "pack" is entirely up to you! Your pup's intuitive quest for dominance, coupled with the fact that it is nearly impossible to look at an adorable Pomeranian pup, with his "puppy-dog" eyes and baby-

PLAY'S THE THING

Teaching the puppy to play with his toys in running and fetching games is an ideal way to help the puppy develop muscle, learn motor skills and bond with you, his owner and master. He also needs to learn how to inhibit his bite reflex and never to use his teeth on people, forbidden objects and other animals in play. Whenever you play with your puppy, you make the rules. This becomes an important message to your puppy in teaching him that you are the pack leader and control everything he does in life. Once your dog accepts you as his leader, your relationship with him will be cemented for life.

fox face, and not cave in, give the pup almost an unfair advantage in getting the upper hand! A pup will definitely test the waters to see what he can and cannot do. Do not give in to those pleading eyes—stand your ground when it comes to disciplining the pup and make sure that all family members do the same. It will only confuse the pup when Mother tells him to get off the sofa when he is used to sitting up there with Father to watch the nightly news. Avoid discrepancies by having all members of the household decide on the rules before the pup even comes home...and be consistent in enforcing them! Early training shapes the dog's personality, so you cannot be unclear in what you expect.

COMMON PUPPY PROBLEMS

The best way to prevent puppy problems is to be proactive in stopping an undesirable behavior as soon as it starts. The old saying "You can't teach an old dog new tricks" does not necessarily hold true, but it *is* true that it is much easier to discourage bad behavior in a young developing pup than to wait until the pup's bad behavior becomes the adult dog's bad habit. There are some problems that are especially prevalent in puppies as they develop.

NIPPING

As puppies start to teethe, they feel the need to sink their teeth into anything available... unfortunately that includes your fingers, arms, hair and toes. You may find this behavior cute for the first five seconds...until you feel just how sharp those puppy teeth are. This is something you want to discourage immediately and consistently with a firm "No!" (or whatever number of firm "Nos" it takes for him to understand that you mean business). Then replace your finger

with an appropriate chew toy. Your Pomeranian does not mean any harm with a friendly nip, but he also does not know how sharp his teeth are.

CRYING/WHINING

Your pup will often cry, whine, whimper, howl or make some type of commotion when he is left alone. This is basically his way of calling out for attention to make sure that you know he

MENTAL AND DENTAL
Toys not only help your puppy get the physical and mental stimulation he needs but also provide a great way to keep his teeth clean. Hard rubber or nylon toys, especially those constructed with grooves, are designed to scrape away plaque, preventing bad breath and gum infection.

CHEWING TIPS

Chewing goes hand in hand with nipping in the sense that a teething puppy is always looking for a way to soothe his aching gums. In this case, instead of chewing on you, he may have taken a liking to your favorite shoe or something else that he should not be chewing. Again, realize that this is a normal canine behavior that does not need to be discouraged, only redirected. Your pup just needs to be taught what is acceptable to chew on and what is off-limits. Consistently tell him "No!" when you catch him chewing on something forbidden and give him a chew toy.

Conversely, praise him when you catch him chewing on something appropriate. In this way, you are discouraging the inappropriate behavior and reinforcing the desired behavior. The puppy's chewing should stop after his adult teeth have come in, but an adult dog continues to chew for various reasons—perhaps because he is bored, needs to relieve tension or just likes to chew. That is why it is important to redirect his chewing when he is still young.

noise he is making is an expression of the anxiety he feels at being alone, so he needs to be taught that being alone is okay. You are not actually training the dog to stop making noise, you are training him to feel comfortable when he is alone and thus removing the need for him to make the noise. This is where the crate with cozy bedding and a toy comes in handy. You want to know that he is safe when you are not there to supervise, and you know that he will be safe in his crate rather than roaming freely about the house. In order for the pup to stay in his crate without making a fuss, he needs to be comfortable in his crate. On that note, it is extremely important that the crate is never used as a form of punishment, or the pup will form a negative association with the crate.

Accustom the pup to the crate in short, gradually increasing time intervals in which you put him in the crate, maybe with a treat, and stay in the room with him. If he cries or makes a fuss, do not go to him, but stay in his sight. Gradually he will realize that staying in his crate is okay without your help, and it will not be so traumatic for him when you are not around. You may want to leave the radio on softly when you leave the house; the sound of human voices may be comforting to him.

is there and that you have not forgotten about him. He feels insecure when he is left alone, when you are out of the house and he is in his crate or when you are in another part of the house and he cannot see you. The

DIETARY AND FEEDING CONSIDERATIONS

Today the choices of food for your Pomeranian are many and varied. There are simply dozens of brands of food in all sorts of flavors and sizes, from puppy diets to those for seniors. There are even hypoallergenic and low-calorie diets available. Because your Pomeranian's food has a bearing on coat, health and temperament, it is essential that the most suitable diet is selected for a Pomeranian of his age. It is fair to say, however, that even dedicated owners can be somewhat perplexed by the enormous range of foods available. Only understanding what is best for your dog will help you reach an informed decision.

Dog foods are produced in three basic types: dry, semi-moist and canned. Dry foods are useful for the cost-conscious for overall they tend to be less expensive than semi-moist or canned. Dry kibble comes in "small-bite" form, which is ideal for the Pom. Dry foods contain the least fat and the most preservatives. In general, canned foods are made up of 60–70% water, while semi-moist ones often contain so much sugar that they are perhaps the least preferred by owners, even though their dogs seem to like them.

When selecting your dog's diet, three stages of development must be considered: the puppy stage, the adult stage and the senior stage.

STORING DOG FOOD

You must store your dry dog food carefully. Open packages of dog food quickly lose their vitamin value, usually within 90 days of being opened. Mold spores and vermin could also contaminate the food.

FOOD PREFERENCE

Selecting the best dry dog food is difficult. There is no majority consensus among veterinary scientists as to the value of nutrient analysis (protein, fat, fiber, moisture, ash, cholesterol, minerals, etc.). All agree that feeding trials are what matter most, but you also have to consider the individual dog. The dog's weight, age and activity level, and what pleases his taste, all must be considered. It is probably best to take the advice of your veterinarian. Every dog's dietary requirements vary, even during the lifetime of a particular dog.

If your dog is fed a good dry food, he does not require supplements of meat or vegetables. Dogs do appreciate a little variety in their diets, so you may choose to stay with the same brand but vary the flavor. Alternatively, you may wish to add a little flavored stock to give a difference to the taste.

The mother's milk is the best food for Pom puppies during the first weeks of their lives.

PUPPY STAGE

Puppies instinctively want to suck milk from their mother's teats, and a normal puppy will exhibit this behavior from just a few moments following birth. If puppies do not attempt to suckle within the first half-hour or so, the breeder encourages them to do so by placing them on the nipples, having selected ones with plenty of milk. This early milk supply is important in providing colostrum to protect the puppies during the first eight to ten weeks of their lives. Although a mother's milk is much better than any milk formula, despite there being some excellent ones available, if the puppies do not feed the breeder will have to feed, them himself. For those with less experience, advice from a veterinarian is important so that not only the right quantity of milk but also that of correct quality is

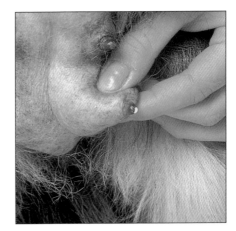

fed at suitably frequent intervals, usually every two hours during the first few days of life.

Puppies should be allowed to nurse from their mothers for about the first six weeks, although from the third or fourth week the breeder will have begun to introduce small portions of suitable solid food. Most breeders like to introduce alternate milk and meat meals initially, building up to weaning time.

By the time the puppies are seven or a maximum of eight weeks old, they should be fully weaned and fed solely on a proprietary puppy food. Selection of the most suitable, good-quality diet at this time is essential, for a puppy's fastest growth rate is during the first year of life. Veterinarians are usually able to offer advice in this regard and, although the frequency of meals will will be reduced over time, only when a

Fatty Risks

Any dog of any breed can suffer from obesity. Studies show that nearly 30% of our dogs are overweight, primarily from high caloric intake and low energy expenditure. The hound and gundog breeds are the most likely affected, and females are at a greater risk of obesity than males. Pet dogs that are neutered are twice as prone to obesity as intact, whole dogs.

Regardless of breed, your dog should have a visible "waist" behind his rib cage and in front of the hind legs. There should be no fatty deposits on his hips or over his rump, and his abdomen should not be extended.

Veterinary specialists link obesity with respiratory problems, cardiac disease and liver dysfunction as well as low sperm count and abnormal estrous cycles in breeding animals. Other complications include musculoskeletal disease (including arthritis), decreased immune competence, diabetes mellitus, hypothroidism, pancreatitis and dermatosis. Other studies have indicated that excess fat leads to heat stress, as obese dogs cannot regulate their body temperatures as well as normal-weight dogs.

Although prevention is the best medicine, don't be discouraged if you find that your dog has developed a problem that requires special veterinary attention. It is possible to tend to his special medical needs. Veterinary specialists focus on areas including cardiology, neurology and oncology. Veterinary medical associations require rigorous training and experience before granting certification in a specialty. Consulting a specialist may offer you greater peace of mind when seeking treatment for your dog.

young dog has reached the age of about 12 months should an adult diet be fed.

Puppy and junior diets should be well balanced for the needs of your dog, so that except in certain circumstances additional vitamins, minerals and proteins will not be required.

GRAIN-BASED DIETS

Some less expensive dog foods are based on grains and other plant proteins. While these products may appear to be attractively priced, many breeders prefer a diet based on animal proteins and believe that they are more conducive to your dog's health. Many grain-based diets rely on soy protein, which may cause flatulence (passing gas).

There are many cases, however, when your dog might require a special diet. These special requirements should only be recommended by your vet.

ADULT DIETS

A dog is considered an adult when he has stopped growing, so in general the diet of a Pomeranian can be changed to an adult one at about 12 months of age. Nevertheless, some Pomeranian owners keep their dogs on puppy food throughout their lives. For such tiny mouths, dry puppy foods are usually more manageable than adult ones, and the protein content is high enough for such an active little dog. Keep in mind that adult foods often come in "small-bite" form.

Again you should rely upon your veterinarian or breeder to recommend an acceptable maintenance diet. There are many specially prepared diets available, but keep in mind that Pomeranians generally require a high-protein diet because of their high levels of activity. They do not usually require such high protein content if they have been spayed or neutered. It is important that you select the food best suited to your dog's needs, for active dogs will require a different diet from those leading very sedate lives. Something else to consider is that too much milk, or

Discuss diet with your breeder. You are well advised to continue using the same brand of food for your pup and to initiate any changes gradually.

other dairy products, can sometimes cause an upset tummy.

SENIOR DIETS

As dogs get older, their metabolism changes. The older dog usually exercises less, moves more slowly and sleeps more. This change in lifestyle and physiological performance requires a change in diet. Since these changes take place slowly,

they might not be recognizable. What is easily recognizable is weight gain. By continuing to feed your dog an adult-maintenance diet when he is slowing down metabolically, your dog will gain weight. Obesity in an older dog compounds the health problems that already accompany old age.

As your dog gets older, few of his organs function up to par. The kidneys slow down and the intestines become less efficient. These age-related factors are best handled with a change in diet and a change in feeding schedule to give smaller portions that are more easily digested.

There is no single best diet for every older dog. While many dogs do well on light or senior

---

TEST FOR PROPER DIET

A good test for proper diet is the color, odor and firmness of your dog's stool. A healthy dog usually produces three semi-hard stools per day. The stools should have no unpleasant odor. They should be the same color from excretion to excretion.

Clean fresh water is essential for every dog.

diets, other dogs do better on special premium diets such as lamb and rice. Be sensitive to your senior Pomeranian's diet and this will help control other problems that may arise with your old friend.

WATER

Just as your dog needs proper nutrition from his food, water is an essential "nutrient" as well. Water keeps the dog's body properly hydrated and promotes

Vitamins Recommended for Dogs

Some breeders and vets recommend the supplementation of vitamins to a dog's diet—others do not. Before embarking on any vitamin program, consult your vet.

Vitamin / Dosage	Food source	Benefits
A / 10,000 IU/week	Eggs, butter, yogurt, meat	Skin, eyes, hind legs, haircoat
B / Varies	Organs, cottage cheese, sardines	Appetite, fleas, heart, skin and coat
C / 2000 mg+	Fruit, legumes, leafy green vegetables	Healing, arthritis, kidneys
D / Varies	Cod liver, cheese, organs, eggs	Bones, teeth, endocrine system
E / 250 IU daily	Leafy green vegetables, meat, wheat germ oil	Skin, muscles, nerves, healing, digestion
F / Varies	Fish oils, raw meat	Heart, skin, coat, fleas
K / Varies	Naturally in body, not through food	Blood clotting

A Worthy Investment

Veterinary studies have proven that a balanced high-quality diet
pays off in your dog's coat quality, behavior and activity level.
Invest in premium brands for the maximum payoff with your dog.

normal function of the body's systems. During housebreaking, it is necessary to keep an eye on how much water your Pomeranian is drinking, but once he is reliably trained he should have access to clean fresh water at all times. Make sure that the dog's water bowl is clean, and change the water at least twice a day. Water should be always available for your dog, especially if you feed dry food.

EXERCISE

Although a Pomeranian is small, all dogs require some form of exercise, regardless of breed. A

The Pom requires regular exercise to maintain his health. Two or three walks per day are ideal for Pom and owner.

sedentary lifestyle is as harmful to a dog as it is to a person. The Pomeranian is an active breed that enjoys exercise, but you don't have to be an Olympic athlete! Regular walks, play sessions in the yard or letting the dog run free in an enclosed area under your supervision are sufficient forms of exercise for the Pomeranian. Bear in mind that an overweight dog should never be suddenly over-exercised; instead, he should be allowed to increase exercise slowly. Not only is exercise essential to keep the dog's body fit, it is essential to his mental well-being. A bored dog will find something to do, which often manifests itself in some type of destructive behavior. In this sense, it is essential for the owner's mental well-being as well!

GROOMING

Because of his double coat, your Pomeranian will need to be groomed regularly, so it is essential that short grooming sessions be introduced from a very early age. From the very beginning, a few minutes each day should be set aside so that your puppy becomes familiar with the process. Set aside a grooming area, ideally a special grooming table with a non-slip surface. In this way, your puppy will learn to associate that place with his grooming sessions and, of course, to behave. If your puppy is taught to behave well for these sessions, grooming will be a pleasure both for the dog and for you for years to come.

Different breeders use varying methods of grooming, and you will undoubtedly eventually find the particular way that suits you best. Poms do not need as much grooming as some of the longer coated breeds, but, nonetheless, the coat does need work and an owner needs to be dedicated to keeping the coat in tip-top condition. You will need to groom your Pom properly at least two or three times each

GROOMING EQUIPMENT

How much grooming equipment you purchase will depend on how much grooming you are going to do. Here are some basics:

- Soft pin brush
- Soft bristle brush
- Wide-toothed comb
- Scissors
- Dog shampoo
- Shower or shower attachment
- Rubber mat
- Towels
- Blow dryer
- Nail clippers
- Liquid ear cleaner
- Tissues/cotton balls
- Tooth-cleaning aids

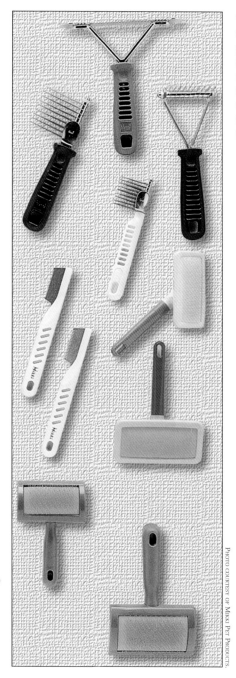

Your Pomeranian will require daily grooming. Your local pet shop will usually have the brushes and other grooming tools necessary for the job.

PHOTO COURTESY OF MIKKI PET PRODUCTS.

A quality pin brush is ideal for daily brushing.

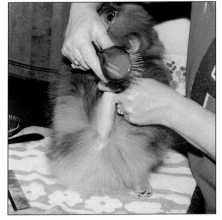

Don't forget to brush through the tail to avoid tangles.

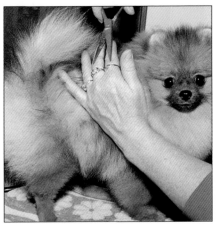

Using a grooming scissors or shears, trim coat ends to create the desired round appearance.

week, and more often than that when the coat is in a stage of change. As a puppy, a Pom is just a little ball of fluff, but owners must be aware that the coat will change considerably as the puppy matures into adulthood.

Once a male Pom has reached the age of about 18 months, his coat is likely to stay more or less the same throughout the year provided he is in good health, but there is likely to be some shedding around spring and autumn. However, the same cannot be said for the coats of unspayed bitches. In conjunction with a bitch's season, hormonal changes can play havoc with her coat, so be prepared! Also, following a litter, it usually takes a good few months for her coat to get back into prime condition.

ROUTINE GROOMING
To keep your Pom looking in prime condition, it is important to keep the coat clean and to groom regularly. Show Poms are usually bathed prior to each show, but those kept as pets are generally washed less often, depending on their lifestyles. Some owners like to bathe every other week but others are happy to bathe every four to six weeks. Bathing can certainly help to prevent skin irritation. Dirt and dust, if allowed to accumulate,

are both drying and abrasive to the coat.

If your show Pom has a softer than desirable coat, it is wise to bathe four or five days before a show, not the night before. And it goes without saying that all grooming equipment must be kept clean and in good condition.

Never groom a coat when completely dry, but use a fine water spray, light coat dressing or even a mixture of conditioner and water (about 1 tablespoon of conditioner to 1/2 quart of water). This will help avoid the removal of too much coat and will also prevent hair breakage.

The coat should be brushed out in sections, using either a bristle (sometimes bristle and nylon) or soft pin brush. Some owners find a slicker brush can also be useful, but these brushes are not ideal because they take out a great deal of coat. A wide-toothed comb can be useful for the finishing touches. On the head, feet and ankles, use a soft brush so that there is no damage to the skin.

The coat should always be groomed in an upwards direction, from tail to neck, the neck ruff being brushed outwards. Breeching at the back should be brushed well away from the anus. The tail plume should also be dealt with most carefully and gently.

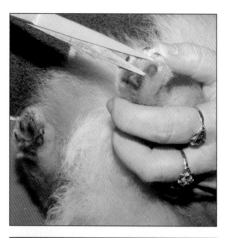

The hair that grows on the bottom of the foot should be trimmed short to prevent matting and discomfort to the dog.

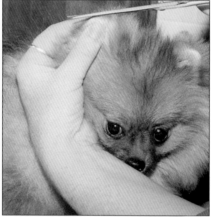

Trimming is done to create a nice blended appearance.

Get in the habit of brushing your Pom's teeth as part of your grooming routine.

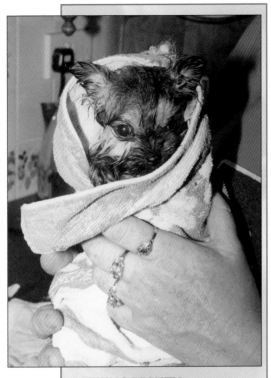

BATHING BEAUTY

Once you are sure that the dog is thoroughly rinsed, squeeze the excess water out of his coat with your hand and dry him with an heavy towel. Once you've absorbed the initial moisture, finish the job by using a blow dryer on his coat. In cold weather, never allow your dog outside with a wet coat.

There are "dry bath" products on the market, which are sprays and powders intended for spot cleaning, that can be used between regular baths if necessary. They are not substitutes for regular baths, but they are easy to use for touch-ups as they do not require rinsing.

TRIMMING

Trimming requires great skill, for over-trimming can spoil both the outline and expression, and under-trimming can look unattractive. It should always be kept in mind that a Pom should resemble a ball, and this picture should stay in your mind while trimming. The chest must be rounded, as must the breechings at the back, and these must blend with the tail plume over the back. Because trimming is a skill, new owners would be well advised to carefully observe more experienced groomers and learn exactly how best to approach this delicate operation.

Doubtless you will pick up some grooming tips from other Pomeranian owners and enthusiasts if you visit shows, and in time you will decide upon the method that best suits you and your dog.

BATHING AND DRYING

As with grooming, every owner has his own preference as to how best to bathe. I like to stand my own dogs on a non-slip mat in the bathtub, though Pomeranians may be bathed in a suitable sink. Start by wetting the coat thoroughly using a shower-hose attachment. It is imperative that you test the water temperature on your own hand, and that you use a good-quality shampoo designed especially for dogs.

Always stroke the shampoo into the coat rather than rub, so as not to create knots, and do take care not to get soap into the eyes. Some like to plug the ears with a cotton ball to avoid water getting inside them, but personally I have never done this; just by taking care in that area, I have never encountered problems. Be sure to rinse thoroughly all shampoo from your Pom's coat. Finally, lift your dog carefully out of the water, wrapped in a warm, clean towel.

Drying is done by applying warm air from a blow dryer, and concentrating on one area at a time, again making sure that the temperature is neither too hot nor too cold. The head is usually left until last. Keep in mind that many dogs do not like warm air blowing directly towards their eyes and noses, so do take this into consideration when angling the dryer.

EAR CLEANING
Ears should be checked weekly for any build-up of dirt, and on a Pomeranian some hair will also grow inside the ears. This should be carefully plucked out with blunt-ended tweezers. Remove only a few hairs at a time and this should be entirely painless. Ears must always be kept clean. This can be done using a special liquid cleaner with cotton balls. Many people

SOAP IT UP
The use of human soap products like shampoo, bubble bath and hand soap can be damaging to a dog's coat and skin. Human products are too strong; they remove the protective oils coating the dog's hair and skin that make him water-resistant. Use only shampoo made especially for dogs. You may like to use a medicated shampoo, which will help to keep external parasites at bay.

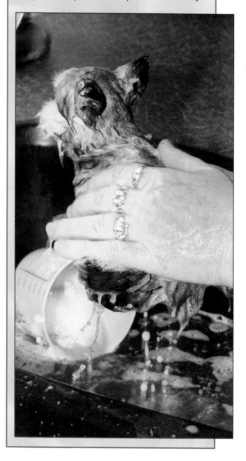

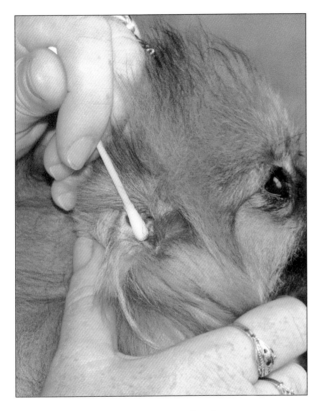

The Pom's ears should be cleaned carefully. Be sure the ears are free of mites. Use a cotton swab with great care.

but long nails can be sharp and scratch someone unintentionally. Also, a long nail has a better chance of ripping and bleeding, or of causing the feet to spread. A good rule of thumb is that if you can hear your dog's nails' clicking on the floor when he walks, his nails are too long.

Before you start cutting, make sure you can identify the "quick" in each nail. The quick is a blood vessel that runs through the center of each nail and grows rather close to the

use cotton swabs, but extreme care must be taken not to delve into the ear canal, as this can cause injury. If his ears have an unusual odor, this is a sure sign of mite infestation or infection, and a signal to have your dog's ears checked by the vet.

NAIL CLIPPING

Your Pomeranian should be accustomed to having his nails trimmed at an early age, since it will be part of your maintenance routine throughout his life. Not only do short nails look nicer,

PEDICURE TIP

A dog that spends a lot of time outside on a hard surface, such as cement or pavement, will have his nails naturally worn down and may not need to have them trimmed as often, except maybe in the colder months when he is not outside as much. Regardless, it is best to get your dog accustomed to the nail-trimming procedure at an early age so that he is used to it. Some dogs are especially sensitive about having their feet touched, but if a dog has experienced it since puppyhood, it should not bother him.

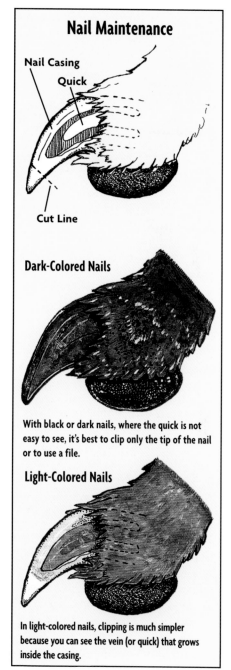

Nail Maintenance

Nail Casing

Quick

Cut Line

Dark-Colored Nails

With black or dark nails, where the quick is not easy to see, it's best to clip only the tip of the nail or to use a file.

Light-Colored Nails

In light-colored nails, clipping is much simpler because you can see the vein (or quick) that grows inside the casing.

Use special dog nail clippers to trim the Pom's nails.

end. It will bleed if accidentally cut, which will be quite painful for the dog as it contains nerve endings. Keep some type of clotting agent on hand, such as a styptic pencil or styptic powder (the type used for shaving). This will stop the bleeding quickly when applied to the end of the cut nail. Do not panic if this happens, just stop the bleeding and talk soothingly to your dog. Once he has calmed down, move on to the next nail. It is better to clip a little at a time, particularly with black-nailed dogs.

Hold your pup steady as you begin trimming his nails; you do not want him to make any sudden movements or run away. Talk to him soothingly and stroke him as you clip. Holding his foot in your hand, simply take off the end of each nail in one quick clip. You can purchase nail clippers that are specially made for dogs; you can probably find them wherever you buy grooming or other pet supplies.

TRAVELING WITH YOUR POMERANIAN

CAR TRAVEL

You should accustom your Pomeranian to riding in a car at an early age. You may or may not take him in the car often, but at the very least he will need to go to the vet and you do not want these trips to be traumatic for the dog or troublesome for

> **TRAVEL TIP**
> Never leave your dog alone in the car. In hot weather, your dog can die from the high temperature inside a closed vehicle; even a car parked in the shade can heat up very quickly. Leaving the window open is dangerous as well since the dog can hurt himself trying to get out.

you. The safest way for a dog to ride in the car is in his crate. If he uses a crate in the house, you can use the same crate for travel.

Put the pup in the crate and see how he reacts. If he seems uneasy, you can have a passenger hold him on his lap while you drive. Another option is a specially made safety harness for dogs, which straps the dog in much like a seat belt. Do not let the dog roam loose in the vehicle—this is very dangerous! If you should stop short, your dog can be thrown and injured. If the dog starts climbing on you and pestering you while you are driving, you will not be able to concentrate on the road. It is an unsafe situation for everyone—human and canine.

For long trips, be prepared to stop to let the dog relieve himself. Bring along whatever you need to clean up after him. You should take along some paper towels and perhaps some old rags for use should he have a potty accident in the car or suffer from motion sickness.

Even though your Pom is tiny, he should never be allowed to roam free in the car. Use the Pom's crate for car travel, even for short distances.

hours prior to checking in so that you minimize his need to relieve himself. Some airlines require you to provide documentation as to when the dog has last been fed. In any case, a light meal is best. For long trips, you will have to attach food and

> **TRAVEL TIP**
> The most extensive travel you do with your dog may be limited to trips to the vet's office—or you may decide to bring him along for long distances when the family goes on vacation. Whichever the case, it is important to consider your dog's safety while traveling.

AIR TRAVEL

Contact your chosen airline before proceeding with your travel plans that include your Pomeranian. The dog will be required to travel in a fiberglass crate and you should always check in advance with the airline regarding specific requirements for the crate's size, type and labeling. To help put the dog at ease, give him one of his favorite toys in the crate. Do not feed the dog for several

Pomeranians enjoy a vacation at the shore as much as the next pampered pet!

water bowls to the dog's crate so that airline employees can tend to him between legs of the trip. Inquire of your chosen airline as to whether your tiny dog can be "carried on" to the passengers' area of the plane. Many airlines permit small dogs to travel in the cabin—in his crate under his owner's seat.

VACATIONS AND BOARDING
So you want to take a family vacation—and you want to include *all* members of the family. You would probably make arrangements for accommodations ahead of time anyway, but this is especially important when traveling with a dog. You do not want to make an overnight stop at the only place around for miles and find out that they do not allow dogs. Also, you do not want to reserve a place for your family without confirming that you are traveling with a dog because, if it is against their policy, you may not have a place to stay.

COLLAR REQUIRED
If your dog gets lost, he is not able to ask for directions home. Identification tags fastened to the collar give important information—the dog's name, the owner's name, the owner's address and a telephone number where the owner can be reached. This makes it easy for whomever finds the dog to contact the owner and arrange to have the dog returned. An added advantage is that a person will be more likely to approach a lost dog who has ID tags on his collar; it tells the person that this is somebody's pet rather than a stray. This is the easiest and fastest method of identification, provided that the tags stay on the collar and the collar stays on the dog.

Select a boarding kennel *before* you actually intend to use it. The kennel must be clean, secure and suitable for a small dog.

Alternatively, if you are traveling and choose not to bring your Pomeranian, you will have to make arrangements for him while you are away. Some options are to take him to a neighbor's house to stay while you are gone, to have a trusted neighbor stay at your house, or to bring your dog to your vet's office for boarding or to a reputable boarding kennel. If you choose to board him at a kennel, you should visit in advance to see the facilities provided, how clean they are and where the dogs are kept. Talk to some of the employees and see how they treat the dogs—do they have experience in dealing with tiny dogs, do they spend time with the dogs, play with them, groom them, exercise them, etc.? Also find out the kennel's policy on vaccinations and what they

TRAVEL TIP

When traveling, never let your dog off-leash in a strange area. Your dog could run away out of fear, decide to chase a passing squirrel or cat or simply want to stretch his legs without restriction—if any of these happen, you might never see your canine friend again.

Your Pom should always wear his collar to which his ID tags and dog licenses are attached.

require. This is for all of the dogs' safety, since when dogs are kept together, there is a greater risk of diseases being passed from dog to dog.

IDENTIFICATION

Your Pomeranian is your valued companion and friend. That is why you always keep a close eye on him and you have made sure that he cannot escape from the yard or wriggle out of his collar and run away from you. However, accidents can happen and there may come a time when your dog unexpectedly becomes separated from you. If this unfortunate event should occur, the first thing on your mind will be finding him. Proper identification, including an ID tag, a tattoo, and possibly tattoo and/or a microchip, will increase the chances of his being returned to you safely and quickly.

IDENTIFICATION OPTIONS

As puppies become more and more expensive, especially those puppies of high quality for showing and/or breeding, they have a greater chance of being stolen. The usual collar dog tag is, of course, easily removed. But there are two more permanent techniques that have become widely used for identification.

The puppy microchip implantation involves the injection of a small microchip, about the size of a corn kernel, under the skin of the dog. If your dog shows up at a clinic or shelter, or is offered for resale under less-than-savory circumstances, he can be positively identified by the microchip. The microchip is scanned, and a registry quickly identifies you as the owner.

Tattooing is done on various parts of the dog, from his belly to his cheeks. The number tattooed can be your telephone number, your dog's registration number or any other number that you can easily memorize. When professional dog thieves see a tattooed dog, they usually lose interest. For the safety of our dogs, no laboratory facility or dog broker will accept a tattooed dog as stock.

Discuss microchipping and tattooing with your veterinarian and breeder. Some vets perform these services on their own premises for a reasonable fee. Be certain that the dog is then properly registered with a legitimate national database to ensure that his ID is effective.

Invest in your Pom's safety as soon as possible. Tattoos and microchips are usually done at an early age. Discuss this with your vet.

TRAINING YOUR
POMERANIAN

Living with an untrained dog is like owning a piano that you do not know how to play—it is a nice object to look at, but it does not do much more than that to bring you pleasure. Now try taking piano lessons, and suddenly the piano comes alive and brings forth magical sounds and rhythms that set your heart singing and your body swaying. The same is true with your Pomeranian. Any dog is a big responsibility and, if not trained sensibly, may develop unacceptable behavior that annoys you or could even cause family friction.

To train your Pomeranian, you may like to enroll in an obedience class. Teach him good manners as you learn how and why he behaves the way he does. Find out how to communicate with your dog and how to recognize and understand his communications with you. Suddenly the dog takes on a new role in your life—he is clever, interesting, well-behaved and fun to be with. He demonstrates his bond of devotion to you daily. In other words, your Pomeranian does wonders for your ego because he constantly reminds you that you are not only his leader, you are his hero!

Those involved with teaching dog obedience and counseling owners about their dogs' behavior have discovered some interesting facts about dog ownership. For example, train-

REAP THE REWARDS
If you start with a normal, healthy dog and give him time, patience and some carefully executed lessons, you will reap the rewards of that training for the life of the dog. And what a life it will be! The two of you will find immeasurable pleasure in the companionship you have built together with love, respect and understanding.

ing dogs when they are puppies results in the highest rate of success in developing well-mannered and well-adjusted adult dogs. Training an older dog, from six months to six years of age, can produce almost equal results, providing that the owner accepts the dog's slower rate of learning capability and is willing to work patiently to help the dog succeed at developing to his fullest potential. Unfortunately, many owners of untrained adult dogs lack the patience factor, so they do not persist until their dogs are successful at learning particular behaviors.

Training a puppy aged 10 to 16 weeks (20 weeks at the most) is like working with a dry sponge in a pool of water. The pup soaks up whatever you show him and constantly looks for more things to do and learn. At this early age, his body is not yet producing hormones, and therein lies the reason for such a high rate of success. Without hormones, he is focused on his owners and not particularly interested in investigating other places, dogs, people, etc. You are his leader: his provider of food, water, shelter and security. He latches onto you and wants to stay close. He will usually follow you from room to room, will not let you out of his sight when you are outdoors with him

PARENTAL GUIDANCE

Training a dog is a life experience. Many parents admit that much of what they know about raising children, they learned from caring for their dogs. Dogs respond to love, fairness and guidance, just as children do. Become a good dog owner and you may become an even better parent.

An adult Pomeranian can be trained with success, as long as the owner is patient and consistent. Adults do not respond to training as readily as puppies, but in time will learn to perform as required.

stranger, he will respond accordingly.

Once the puppy begins to produce hormones, his natural curiosity emerges and he begins to investigate the world around him. It is at this time when you may notice that the untrained dog begins to wander away from you and even ignore your commands to stay close. When this behavior becomes a problem, the owner has two choices: get rid of the dog or train him. It is strongly urged that you choose the latter option.

There usually will be classes within a reasonable distance from your home, but you can also do a lot to train your dog yourself. Sometimes there are classes available but the tuition is too costly. Whatever the circumstances, the solution to the problem of training your Pom without formal obedience classes lies within the pages of this book.

This chapter is devoted to helping you train your Pomeranian at home. If the recommended procedures are followed faithfully, you may expect positive results that will prove rewarding to both you and your dog.

Whether your new charge is a puppy or a mature adult, the methods of teaching and the techniques we use in training basic behaviors are the same. After all, no dog, whether puppy

and will respond in like manner to the people and animals you encounter. If you greet a friend warmly, he will be happy to greet the person as well. If, however, you are hesitant even anxious about the approach of a

THINK BEFORE YOU BARK
Dogs are sensitive to their masters' moods and emotions. Use your voice wisely when communicating with your dog. Never raise your voice at your dog unless you are trying to correct him. "Barking" at your dog can become as meaningless as "dogspeak" is to you.

or adult, likes harsh or inhumane methods. All creatures, however, respond favorably to gentle motivational methods and sincere praise and encouragement. Now let us get started.

HOUSEBREAKING

You can train a puppy to relieve himself wherever you choose, but this must be somewhere suitable. You should bear in mind from the outset that when your puppy is old enough to go out in public places, any canine deposits must be removed at once. You will always have to carry with you a small plastic bag or "poop-scoop."

Outdoor training includes such surfaces as grass, soil or earth and cement. Indoor training usually means training your dog to newspaper.

MEALTIME

Mealtime should be a peaceful time for your Pomeranian. Do not put his food and water bowls in a high-traffic area in the house. For example, give him his own little corner of the kitchen where he can eat undisturbed and where he will not be underfoot. Do not allow small children or other family members to disturb the dog when he is eating.

Keeping the student's attention is half the battle when training a young Pomeranian.

When deciding on the surface and location that you will want your Pomeranian to use, be sure it is going to be permanent. Training your dog to grass and then changing your

FEAR AGGRESSION

Pups who are subjected to physical abuse during training commonly end up with behavioral problems as adults. One common result of abuse is fear aggression, in which a dog will lash out, bare his teeth, snarl and finally bite someone by whom he feels threatened. For example, your daughter may be playing with the dog one afternoon. As they play hide-and-seek, she backs the dog into a corner and, as she attempts to tease him playfully, he bites her hand. Examine the cause of this behavior. Did your daughter ever hit the dog? Did someone who resembles your daughter hit or scream at the dog?

Fortunately, fear aggression is relatively easy to correct. Have your daughter engage in only positive activities with the dog, such as feeding, petting and walking. She should not give any corrections or negative feedback. If the dog still growls or cowers away from her, allow someone else to accompany them. After approximately one week, the dog should feel that he can rely on her for many positive things, and he will also be prevented from reacting fearfully towards anyone who might resemble her.

mind two months later is extremely difficult for both dog and owner.

Next, choose the command you will use each and every time you want your puppy to void. "Be quick," "Hurry up" and "Potty" are examples of commands commonly used by dog owners. Get in the habit of giving the puppy your chosen relief command before you take him out. That way, when he becomes an adult, you will be able to determine if he wants to go out when you ask him. A confirmation will be signs of interest, such as wagging his tail, watching you intently, going to the door, etc.

Puppy's Needs

The puppy needs to relieve himself after play periods, after each meal, after he has been sleeping and any time he indicates that he is looking for a place to urinate or defecate. The urinary and intestinal tract muscles of very young puppies are not fully developed. Therefore, like human babies, puppies need to relieve themselves frequently.

Take your puppy out often—every hour for a ten-week-old, for example, and always immediately after sleeping and eating. The older the puppy, the less often he will need to relieve himself. Finally, as a mature healthy adult, he will require only three to five relief trips per day.

Housing

Since the types of housing and control you provide for your puppy have a direct relationship on the success of house-training, we consider the various aspects of both before we begin training. Bringing a new puppy home and turning him loose in your house can be compared to turning a child loose in a sports arena and telling the child that the place is all his! The sheer enormity of the place would be too much for him to handle.

Instead, offer the puppy clearly defined areas where he can play, sleep, eat and live. A room of the house where the family gathers is the most obvious choice. Puppies are social animals and need to feel a part of the pack right from the start. Hearing your voice, watching you while you are doing things and smelling you nearby are all positive reinforcers that he is now a member of your pack. Usually a family room, the kitchen or a nearby adjoining breakfast area is ideal for providing safety and security for both puppy and owner.

Within that room, there should be a smaller area that the puppy can call his own. An alcove, a wire or fiberglass dog crate or a gated (not boarded!) corner from which he can view the activities of his new family will be fine. The size of the area or crate is the key factor here. The area must be large enough for the puppy to lie down and stretch out as well as stand up

SAFETY FIRST
While it may seem that the most important things to your dog are eating, sleeping and chewing the upholstery on your furniture, his first concern is actually safety. The domesticated dogs we keep as companions have the same pack instinct as their ancestors who ran free thousands of years ago. Because of this pack instinct, your dog wants to know that he and his pack are not in danger of being harmed, and that his pack has a strong, capable leader. You must establish yourself as the leader early on in your relationship. That way your dog will trust that you will take care of him and the pack, and he will accept your commands without question.

There is no better housing for your Pom than a small crate.

without rubbing his head on top, yet small enough so that he cannot relieve himself at one end and sleep at the other without coming into contact with his droppings. The designated area should be lined with clean bedding and a toy. Water must always be available, in a non-spill container, but remember— what goes in must come out!

Dogs are, by nature, clean animals and will not remain close to their relief areas unless forced to do so. In those cases, they then become dirty dogs and usually remain that way for life.

CONTROL

By *control*, we mean helping the puppy to create a lifestyle pattern that will be compatible to that of his human pack *(you!)*. Just as we guide little

PAPER CAPER
Never line your pup's sleeping area with newspaper. Puppy litters are usually raised on newspaper and, once in your home, the puppy will immediately associate newspaper with voiding. Never put newspaper on any floor while house-training, as this will only confuse the puppy. If you are paper-training him, use paper in his designated relief area only. Finally, restrict water intake after evening meals. Offer a few licks at a time—never let a young puppy gulp water after meals.

children to learn our way of life, we must show the puppy when it is time to play, eat, sleep, exercise and even entertain himself.

Your puppy should always sleep in his crate. He should also learn that, during times of household confusion and excessive human activity such as at breakfast when family members are preparing for the day, he can play by himself in relative safety and comfort in his designated area. Each time you leave

CANINE DEVELOPMENT SCHEDULE

It is important to understand how and at what age a puppy develops into adulthood. If you are a puppy owner, consult the following Canine Development Schedule to determine the stage of development your puppy is currently experiencing. This knowledge will help you as you work with the puppy in the weeks and months ahead.

Period	Age	Characteristics
FIRST TO THIRD	**BIRTH TO SEVEN WEEKS**	Puppy needs food, sleep and warmth, and responds to simple and gentle touching. Needs mother for security and disciplining. Needs littermates for learning and interacting with other dogs. Pup learns to function within a pack and learns pack order of dominance. Begin socializing pup with adults and children for short periods. Pup begins to become aware of his environment.
FOURTH	**EIGHT TO TWELVE WEEKS**	Brain is fully developed. Needs socializing with outside world. Remove from mother and littermates. Needs to change from canine pack to human pack. Human dominance necessary. Fear period occurs between 8 and 12 weeks. Avoid fright and pain.
FIFTH	**THIRTEEN TO SIXTEEN WEEKS**	Training and formal obedience should begin. Less association with other dogs, more with people, places, situations. Period will pass easily if you remember this is pup's change-to-adolescence time. Be firm and fair. Flight instinct prominent. Permissiveness and over-disciplining can do permanent damage. Praise for good behavior.
JUVENILE	**FOUR TO EIGHT MONTHS**	Another fear period about 7 to 8 months of age. It passes quickly, but be cautious of fright and pain. Sexual maturity reached. Dominant traits established. Dog should understand sit, down, come and stay by now.

NOTE: THESE ARE APPROXIMATE TIME FRAMES. ALLOW FOR INDIVIDUAL DIFFERENCES IN PUPPIES.

the puppy alone, he should understand exactly where he is to stay. Puppies are chewers. They cannot tell the difference between things like lamp cords, television wires, shoes, table legs, etc. Chewing into a television wire, for example, can be fatal to the puppy, while a shorted wire can start a fire in the house.

If the puppy chews on a chair when he is alone, you will probably discipline him angrily when you get home. Thus, he makes the association that your coming home means he is going to be punished. (He will not remember chewing the chair and is incapable of making the association of the discipline with his naughty deed.)

Times of excitement, such as visits from friends, family parties, etc., can be fun for the puppy, providing he can view the activities from the security of his designated area. He is not underfoot and he is not being fed all sorts of tidbits that will probably cause him stomach

A wire crate, completely fitted with a non-spill water dish, is ideal for the Pomeranian.

> **THE GOLDEN RULE**
> The golden rule of dog training is simple. For each "question" (command), there is only one correct answer (reaction). One command = one reaction. Keep practicing the command until the dog reacts correctly without hesitating. Be repetitive but not monotonous. Dogs get bored just as people do!

distress, yet he still feels a part of the fun.

SCHEDULE
A puppy should be taken to his relief area each time he is released from his designated area, after meals, after play sessions, when he first awakens in the morning (at age eight weeks, this can mean 5 a.m.!) or any time he indicates that he's ready "to go" by circling or sniffing busily—do not misinterpret these signs. For a puppy less than 12 weeks of age, a routine of taking him out every hour is necessary. As the puppy grows, he will be able to wait for longer periods of time.

Keep trips to his relief area short. Stay no more than five or six minutes and then return to the house. If he goes during that time, praise him lavishly and take him indoors immediately. If he does not, but he has an accident when you go back indoors, pick him up immediately, say "No! No!" and return to his relief area. Wait a few minutes, then return to the house again. Never hit a puppy or put his face in urine or excrement when he has an accident!

Once indoors, put the puppy in his crate until you have had time to clean up his accident. Then release him to the family area and watch him more closely than before. Chances are, his accident was a result of your not picking up his signal or waiting too long before offering him the opportunity to relieve himself. Never hold a grudge against the puppy for accidents.

Let the puppy learn that going outdoors means it is time to relieve himself, not play. Once trained, he will be able to play indoors and out and still differentiate between the times for play versus the times for relief.

Help the puppy develop regular hours for naps, being

alone, playing by himself and just resting, all in his crate. Encourage him to entertain himself while you are busy with your activities. Let him learn that having you near is comforting, but it is not your main purpose in life to provide him with undivided attention.

Each time you put your puppy in his own area, use the same command, whatever suits best. Soon, he will run to his crate or special area when he hears you say those words.

Crate training provides safety for you, the puppy and the home. It also provides the puppy with a feeling of security, and that helps the puppy achieve self-confidence and clean habits.

Remember that one of the primary ingredients in house-

House-training males is often more difficult than dealing with females. Unaltered males may mark their territory even inside the home. Neutering pets of both sexes is strongly encouraged.

CALM DOWN

Dogs will do anything for your attention. If you reward the dog when he is calm and resting, you will develop a well-mannered dog. If, on the other hand, you greet your dog excitedly and encourage him to wrestle with you, the dog will greet you the same way and you will have a hyperactive dog on your hands.

HOW MANY TIMES A DAY?

AGE	RELIEF TRIPS
To 14 weeks	10
14–22 weeks	8
22–32 weeks	6
Adulthood	4
(dog stops growing)	

These are estimates, of course, but they are a guide to the *minimum* number of opportunities a dog should have each day to relieve himself.

training your puppy is control. Regardless of your lifestyle, there will always be occasions when you will need to have a place where your dog can stay and be happy and safe. Crate training is the answer for now and in the future.

In conclusion, a few key elements are really all you need for a successful house-training method—consistency, frequency, praise, control and supervision. By following these procedures with a normal, healthy puppy, you and the puppy will soon be past the stage of accidents and ready to move on to a clean and rewarding life together.

ROLES OF DISCIPLINE, REWARD AND PUNISHMENT

Discipline, training one to act in accordance with rules, brings order to life. It is as simple as that. Without discipline, particularly in a group society, chaos reigns supreme and the group will eventually perish. Humans and canines are social animals and need some form of discipline in order to function effectively. They must procure food, reproduce to keep their species going and protect their home base and their young.

If there were no discipline in the lives of social animals, they would eventually die from starvation and/or predation by other stronger animals. In the case of domestic canines, dogs need discipline in their lives in order to understand how their pack (you and other family members) functions and how they must act in order to survive.

A large humane society in a highly populated area recently surveyed dog owners regarding their satisfaction with their relationships with their dogs. People who had trained their dogs were 75% more satisfied with their pets than those who had never trained their dogs.

Dr. Edward Thorndike, a noted psychologist, established *Thorndike's Theory of Learning*, which states that a behavior that results in a pleasant event tends to be repeated. Likewise, a behavior that results in an unpleasant event tends not to be repeated. It is this theory on

THE SUCCESS METHOD

Success that comes by luck is usually short-lived. Success that comes by well-thought-out proven methods is often more easily achieved and permanent. This is the Success Method. It is designed to give you, the puppy owner, a simple yet proven way to help your puppy develop clean living habits and a feeling of security in his new environment.

6 Steps to Successful Crate Training

1 Tell the puppy "Crate time!" and place him in the crate with a small treat (a piece of cheese or half of a biscuit). Let him stay in the crate for five minutes while you are in the same room. Then release him and praise lavishly. Never release him when he is fussing. Wait until he is quiet before you let him out.

2 Repeat Step 1 several times a day.

3 The next day, place the puppy in the crate as before. Let him stay there for ten minutes. Do this several times.

4 Continue building time in five-minute increments until the puppy stays in his crate for 30 minutes with you in the room. Always take him to his relief area after prolonged periods in his crate.

5 Now go back to Step 1 and let the puppy stay in his crate for five minutes, this time while you are out of the room.

6 Once again, build crate time in five-minute increments with you out of the room. When the puppy will stay willingly in his crate (he may even fall asleep!) for 30 minutes with you out of the room, he will be ready to stay in it for several hours at a time.

A crate, toys and other necessities should be in your home before the Pom puppy arrives.

with it. Therefore, a behavior that results in an unpleasant event tends not to be repeated.

A good example of a dog learning the hard way is the dog who chases the house cat. He is told many times to leave the cat alone, yet he persists in teasing the cat. Then, one day he begins chasing the cat but the cat turns and swipes a claw across the dog's face, leaving him with a painful gash on his nose. The final result is that the dog stops chasing the cat.

TRAINING EQUIPMENT

COLLAR AND LEASH
For a Pomeranian the collar and leash that you use for training must be one with which you are easily able to work, not too heavy for the dog and perfectly safe.

which training methods are based today. For example, if you manipulate a dog to perform a specific behavior and reward him for doing it, he is likely to do it again because he enjoyed the end result.

Occasionally, punishment, a penalty inflicted for an offense, is necessary. The best type of punishment often comes from an outside source. For example, a child is told not to touch the stove because he may get burned. He disobeys and touches the stove. In doing so, he receives a burn. From that time on, he respects the heat of the stove and avoids contact

CONSISTENCY PAYS OFF
Dogs need consistency in their feeding schedule, exercise and relief visits, and in the verbal commands you use. If you use "Stay" on Monday and "Stay here, please" on Tuesday, you will confuse your dog. Don't demand perfect behavior during training sessions and then let him have the run of the house the rest of the day. Above all, lavish praise on your pet consistently every time he does something right. The more he feels he is pleasing you, the more willing he will be to learn.

THE CLEAN LIFE

By providing sleeping and resting quarters that fit the dog, and offering frequent opportunities to relieve himself outside his quarters, the puppy quickly learns that the outdoors (or the newspaper if you are training him to paper) is the place to go when he needs to urinate or defecate. It also reinforces his innate desire to keep his sleeping quarters clean. This, in turn, helps develop the muscle control that will eventually produce a dog with clean living habits.

TREATS

Have a bag of treats on hand. Something nutritious and easy to swallow works best. Use a soft treat, a chunk of cheese or a piece of cooked chicken rather than a dry biscuit. By the time the dog has finished chewing a dry treat, he will forget why he is being rewarded in the first place! A note of interest: using food rewards will not teach a dog to beg at the table—the only way to teach a dog to beg at the table is to give him food from the table. In training, rewarding the dog with a food treat will help him associate praise and the treats with learning new behaviors that obviously please his owner.

TRAINING BEGINS: ASK THE DOG A QUESTION

In order to teach your dog anything, you must first get his attention. After all, he cannot learn anything if he is looking away from you with his mind on something else.

To get his attention, ask him "School?" and immediately walk over to him and give him a treat as you tell him "Good

Pomeranians thrive on praise and encouragement. Challenge your Pomeranian and he will respond with enthusiasm. Give him a reason to please you.

PLAN TO PLAY

The puppy should also have regular play and exercise sessions when he is with you or a family member. Exercise for a very young puppy can consist of a short walk around the house or yard. Playing can include fetching games with a large ball or a special toy. (All puppies teethe and need soft things upon which to chew.) Remember to restrict play periods to indoors within his living area (the family room, for example) until he is completely house-trained.

dog." Wait a minute or two and repeat the routine, this time with a treat in your hand as you approach within a foot of the dog. Do not go directly to him, but stop about a foot short of him and hold out the treat as you ask "School?" He will see you approaching with a treat in your hand and most likely begin walking toward you. As you meet, give him the treat and praise again.

The third time, ask the question, have a treat in your hand and walk only a short distance toward the dog so that he must walk almost all the way to you. As he reaches you, give him the treat and praise again.

By this time, the dog will probably be getting the idea that if he pays attention to you, especially when you ask that question, it will pay off in treats and enjoyable activities for him. In other words, he learns that "school" means doing things with you that result in treats and positive attention for him.

Remember that the dog does not understand your verbal language, he only recognizes sounds. Your question translates to a series of sounds for him, and those sounds become the signal to go to you and pay attention; if he does, he will get to interact with you plus receive treats and praise.

THE BASIC COMMANDS

TEACHING SIT

Now that you have the dog's attention, attach his leash and hold it in your left hand and a food treat in your right. Place your food hand at the dog's nose and let him lick the treat but not take it from you. Say "Sit" and slowly raise your food hand from in front of the dog's nose to up over his head so that he is looking at the ceiling. As he bends his head upward, he will have to bend his knees to maintain his balance. As he bends his knees, he will assume a sit position. At that point, release the food treat and praise lavishly with comments such as "Good dog! Good sit!" Remember to always praise enthusiastically, because dogs relish verbal

CHOOSE AN APPROPRIATE COLLAR

The **BUCKLE COLLAR** is the standard collar used for everyday purposes. Be sure that you adjust the buckle on growing puppies. Check it every day. It can become too tight overnight! These collars can be made of leather or nylon. Attach your dog's identification tags to this collar.

The **CHOKE COLLAR** is constructed of highly polished steel so that it slides easily through the stainless steel loop. The idea is that the dog controls the pressure around his neck and he will stop pulling if the collar becomes uncomfortable. Chain choke collars are *not* appropriate for coated breeds like the Pom.

The **HALTER** is for a trained dog that has to be restrained to prevent running away, chasing a cat and the like. Considered the most humane of all collars, it is frequently used on smaller dogs on which collars are not comfortable.

TRAINING RULES

If you want to be successful in training your dog, you have four rules to obey yourself:

1. Develop an understanding of how a dog thinks.
2. Do not blame the dog for lack of communication.
3. Define your dog's personality and act accordingly.
4. Have patience and be consistent.

praise from their owners and feel so proud of themselves whenever they accomplish a behavior.

You will not use food forever in getting the dog to obey your commands. Food is only used to teach new behaviors and, once the dog knows what you want when you give a specific command, you will wean him off the food treats but

Attentive, bright and somewhat independent, the Pomeranian makes a rewarding obedience partner for the right owner.

still maintain the verbal praise. After all, you will always have your voice with you, and there will be many times when you have no food rewards but expect the dog to obey.

TEACHING DOWN

Teaching the down exercise is easy when you understand how the dog perceives the down position, and it is very difficult when you do not. Dogs perceive the down position as a submissive one; therefore, teaching the down exercise using a forceful method can sometimes make the dog develop such a fear of the down that he either runs away when you say "Down" or he attempts to snap at the person who tries to force him down.

Have the dog sit close alongside your left leg, facing in the same direction as you are. Hold the leash in your left hand and a food treat in your right. Now place your left hand lightly on the top of the dog's shoulders where they meet above the spinal cord. Do not push down on the dog's shoulders; simply rest your left hand there so you can guide the dog to lie down close to your left leg rather than to swing away from your side when he drops.

Now place the food hand at the dog's nose, say "Down" very softly (almost a whisper) and slowly lower the food hand to the dog's front feet. When the food hand reaches the floor, begin moving it forward along the floor in front of the dog. Keep talking softly to the dog, saying things like, "Do you want this treat? You can do this, good dog." Your reassuring tone of voice will help calm the dog as he tries to follow the food hand in order to get the treat.

When the dog's elbows touch the floor, release the food and praise softly. Try to get the dog to maintain that down position for several seconds before you let him sit up again. The goal here is to get the dog to settle down and not feel threatened in the down position.

TEACHING STAY

It is easy to teach the dog to stay in either a sit or a down position. Again, we use food and

---

LANGUAGE BARRIER

Dogs do not understand our language and have to rely on tone of voice more than just words or sound. They can be trained to react to a certain sound, at a certain volume. If you say "No, Oliver" in a very soft, pleasant voice, it will not have the same meaning as "No, Oliver!!" when you raise your voice. You should never use the dog's name during a reprimand, just the command "No! " You never want the dog to associate his name with a negative experience or reprimand.

PRACTICE MAKES PERFECT!

• Have training lessons with your dog every day in several short segments— three to five times a day for a few minutes at a time is ideal.

• Do not have long practice sessions. The dog will become easily bored.

• Never practice when you are tired, ill, worried or in an otherwise negative mood. This will transmit to the dog and may have an adverse effect on his performance.

   Think fun, short and above all *positive!* End each session on a high note, rather than a failed exercise, and make sure to give a lot of praise. Enjoy the training and help your dog enjoy it, too.

praise during the teaching process as we help the dog to understand exactly what it is that we are expecting him to do.

To teach the sit/stay, start with the dog sitting on your left side as before and hold the leash in your left hand. Have a food treat in your right hand and place your food hand at the dog's nose. Say "Stay" and step out on your right foot to stand directly in front of the dog, toe to toe, as he licks and nibbles the treat. Be sure to keep his head facing upward to maintain the sit position. Count to five and then swing around to stand next to the dog again with him on your left. As soon as you get back to the original position, release the food and praise lavishly.

To teach the down/stay, do the down as previously described. As soon as the dog lies down, say "Stay" and step out on your right foot just as you did in the sit/stay. Count to five and then return to stand beside the dog with him on your left side. Release the treat and praise as always.

Within a week or ten days, you can begin to add a bit of distance between you and your dog when you leave him. When you do, use your left hand open with the palm facing the dog as a stay signal, much the same as the hand signal a police officer uses to stop traffic at an inter-section. Hold the food treat in your right hand as before, but this time the food is not touch-ing the dog's nose. He will watch the food hand and quickly learn that he is going to get that treat as soon as you return to his side.

When you can stand 3 feet away from your dog for 30 seconds, you can then begin

DOUBLE JEOPARDY
A dog in jeopardy never lies down. He stays alert on his feet because instinct tells him that he may have to run away or fight for his survival. Therefore, if a dog feels threatened or anxious, he will not lie down. Consequently, it is important to keep the dog calm and relaxed as he learns the down exercise.

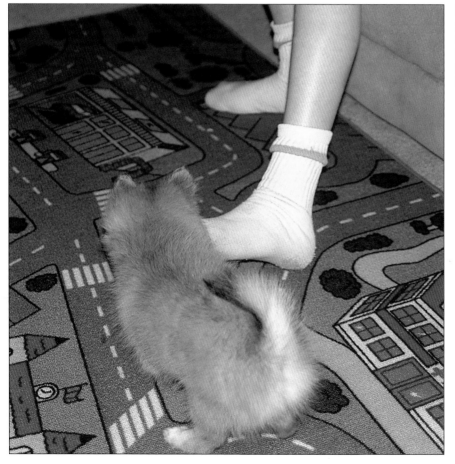

Training means molding all facets of your Pom's behavior, including discouraging bad habits like nipping.

building time and distance in both stays. Eventually, the dog can be expected to remain in the stay position for prolonged periods of time until you return to him or call him to you. Always praise lavishly when he stays.

TEACHING COME

If you make teaching "come" a fun experience, you should never have a student that does not love the game or that fails to come when called. The secret, it seems, is never to teach the word "come."

At times when an owner most wants his dog to come when called, the owner is likely to be upset or anxious and he allows these feelings to come through in the tone of his voice when he calls his dog. Hearing that desperation in his owner's voice, the dog fears the results of going to him and therefore either disobeys outright or runs in the opposite direction. The secret, therefore, is to teach the dog a game and, when you want him to come to you, simply play the game. It is practically a no-fail solution!

To begin, have several members of your family take a few food treats and each go into a different room in the house. Take turns calling the dog, and each person should celebrate the dog's finding him with a treat and lots of happy praise.

When a person calls the dog, he is actually inviting the dog to find him and get a treat as a reward for "winning."

A few turns of the "Where are you?" game and the dog will understand that everyone is playing the game and that each person has a big celebration awaiting the dog's success at locating them. Once the dog learns to love the game, simply calling out "Where are you?" will bring him running from wherever he is when he hears that all-important question.

THE STUDENT'S STRESS TEST

During training sessions, you must be able to recognize signs of stress in your dog such as:

- tucking his tail between his legs
- lowering his head
- shivering or trembling
- standing completely still or running away
- panting and/or salivating
- avoiding eye contact
- flattening his ears back
- urinating submissively
- rolling over and lifting a leg
- grinning or baring teeth
- aggression when restrained

If your four-legged student displays these signs, he may just be nervous or intimidated. The training session may have been too lengthy, with not enough praise and affirmation. Stop for the day and try again tomorrow.

FETCH!

Play fetching games with your puppy in an enclosed area where he can retrieve his toy and bring it back to you. Always use a toy or object designated just for this purpose. Never use a shoe, sock or other item he may later confuse with those in your closet or underneath your chair.

The come command is recognized as one of the most important things to teach a dog, but there are trainers who work with thousands of dogs and never teach the actual word "come." Yet these dogs will race to respond to a person who uses the dog's name followed by "Where are you?" For example, a woman has a 12-year-old companion dog who went blind, but who never fails to locate her owner when asked, "Where are you?"

Children particularly love to play this game with their dogs. Children can hide in smaller places like a shower or bathtub, behind a bed or under a table.

Responsive and intelligent, the Pomeranian makes a worthy student. Do not overwhelm the dog with too many commands or overly long lessons, lest he lose heart!

TUG OF WALK?

If you begin teaching the heel by taking long walks and letting the dog pull you along, he misinterprets this action as an acceptable form of taking a walk. When you pull back on the leash to counteract his pulling, he reads that tug as a signal to pull even harder!

The dog needs to work a little bit harder to find these hiding places but, when he does, he loves to celebrate with a treat and a tussle with a favorite youngster.

TEACHING HEEL

Heeling means that the dog walks beside the owner without pulling. It takes time and patience on the owner's part to succeed at teaching the dog that he (the owner) will not proceed unless the dog is walking calmly beside him. Pulling out ahead on the leash is definitely not acceptable.

Begin with holding the leash in your left hand as the dog sits beside your left leg. Move the loop end of the leash to your right hand but keep your left hand short on the leash so it keeps the dog in close next to you.

Say "Heel" and step forward on your left foot. Keep the dog close to you and take three steps. Stop and have the dog sit next to you in what we now call the heel position. Praise verbally, but do not touch the dog. Hesitate a moment and begin again with "Heel," taking three steps and stopping, at which point the dog is told to sit again.

Your goal here is to have the dog walk those three steps without pulling on the leash. When he will walk calmly beside you for three steps without pulling, increase the number of steps you take to five. When he will walk politely beside you while you take five steps, you can increase the length of your walk to ten steps. Keep increasing the length of your stroll until the dog will walk quietly beside you without pulling as long as you want him to heel. When you stop heeling, indicate to the dog that the exercise is over by verbally praising as you pet him and say "OK, good dog." The "OK" is used as a release word, meaning that the exercise is finished and the dog is free to relax.

If you are dealing with a dog who insists on tugging on the leash, simply "put on your brakes" and stand your ground until the dog realizes that the two of you are not going anywhere until he is beside you and moving at your pace, not his. It may take some time just standing there to convince the

"My kingdom for a liver treat!" All dogs respond to the persuasive fragrance of smoked meat! Use treats wisely in getting your Pom to obey your commands.

dog that you are the leader and you will be the one to decide on the direction and speed of your travel.

Each time the dog looks up at you or slows down to give a slack leash between the two of you, quietly praise him and say "Good heel. Good dog." Eventually, the dog will begin to respond and within a few days he will be walking politely beside you without pulling on the leash. At first, the training sessions should be kept short and very positive; soon the dog will be able to walk nicely with you for increasingly longer distances. Remember also to give the dog free time and the opportunity to run and play when you have finished heel practice.

HEELING WELL
Teach your dog to heel in an enclosed area. Once you think the dog will obey reliably and you want to attempt advanced obedience exercises such as off-leash heeling, test him in a fenced-in area so he cannot run away.

WEANING OFF FOOD IN TRAINING
Food is used in training new behaviors. Once the dog understands what behavior goes with

Smiling Poms make a pretty portrait; with an owner's guidance, their behavior can be picture-perfect, too.

a specific command, it is time to start weaning him off the food treats. At first, give a treat after each exercise. Then, start to give a treat only after every other exercise. Mix up the times when you offer a food reward and the times when you only offer praise so that the dog will never know when he is going to receive both food and praise and when he is going to receive only praise. This is called a variable ratio reward system and it proves successful because there is always the chance that the owner will produce a treat, so the dog never stops trying for that reward. No matter what, *always* give verbal praise.

HOW TO WEAN THE "TREAT HOG"

If you have trained your dog by rewarding him with a treat each time he performs a command, he may soon decide that, without the treat, he won't sit, stay or come. The best way to fix this problem is to start asking your dog to do certain commands twice before being rewarded. Slowly increase the number of commands given and then vary the number: three sits and a treat one day, five sits for a biscuit the next day, etc. Your dog will soon realize that there is no set number of sits before he gets his reward and he'll likely do it the first time you ask in the hope of being rewarded sooner rather than later.

HELPING PAWS

Your dog may not be the next Lassie, but every pet has the potential to do some tricks well. Identify his natural talents and hone them. Is your dog always happy and upbeat? Teach him to wag his tail or give you his paw on command. Real homebodies can be trained to do household chores, such as carrying your slippers or retrieving the morning paper.

OBEDIENCE CLASSES

It is a good idea to enroll in an obedience class if one is available in your area. If yours is a show dog, handling classes would be more appropriate. Many areas have dog clubs that offer basic obedience training as well as preparatory classes for obedience competition. There are also local dog trainers who offer similar classes.

At obedience trials, dogs can earn titles at various levels of competition. The beginning levels of competition include basic behaviors such as sit, down, heel, etc. The more advanced levels of competition include jumping, retrieving, scent discrimination and signal work. The advanced levels require a dog and owner to put a lot of time and effort into their training and the titles that can be earned at these levels of competition are very prestigious.

OTHER ACTIVITIES FOR LIFE

Whether a dog is trained in the structured environment of a class or alone with his owner at home, there are many activities that can bring enjoyment and rewards to both owner and dog once they have mastered basic control.

Teaching the dog to help out around the home or in the garden provides great satisfaction to both dog and owner. In addition, the dog's help makes life a little easier for his owner and raises his stature as a valued companion to his family. It helps give the dog a purpose by occupying his mind and providing an outlet for his energy.

If you are interested in participating in organized competition with your Pomeranian, there are activities other than obedience in which you and your dog can become involved. Agility is a popular sport where dogs run through an obstacle course that includes various jumps, tunnels and other exercises to test the dog's speed and coordination. The owners run through the course beside their dogs to give commands and to guide them through the course. Although competitive, the focus is on fun—it's fun to do, fun to watch and great exercise.

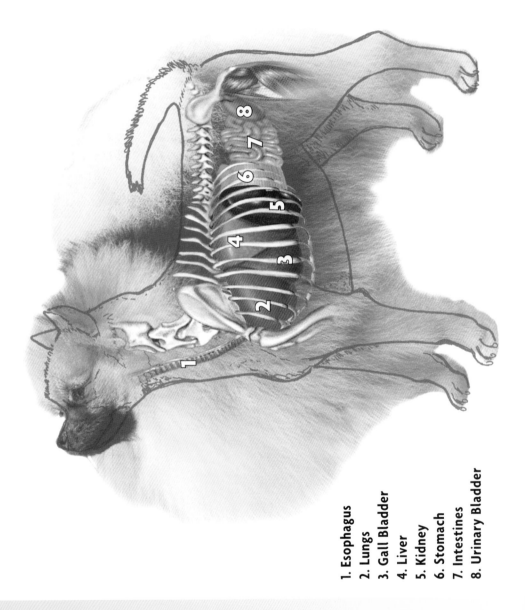

1. Esophagus
2. Lungs
3. Gall Bladder
4. Liver
5. Kidney
6. Stomach
7. Intestines
8. Urinary Bladder

Internal Organs of the Pomeranian

POMERANIAN

Dogs suffer from many of the same physical illnesses as people. They might even share many of the same psychological problems. Since people usually know more about human diseases than canine maladies, many of the terms used in this chapter will be familiar but not necessarily those used by veterinarians. We will use the term *x-ray*, instead of the more acceptable term *radiograph*. We will also use the familiar term *symptoms* even though dogs don't have symptoms, which are verbal descriptions of the patient's feelings; dogs have *clinical signs*. Since dogs can't speak, we have to look for clinical signs...but we still use the term *symptoms* in this book.

As a general rule, medicine is *practiced*. That term is not arbitrary. Medicine is a constantly changing art as we learn more and more about genetics, electronic aids (like CAT scans and MRIs) and daily laboratory advances. There are many dog maladies, like canine hip dysplasia, which are not universally treated in the same manner. Some veterinarians opt for surgery more often than others do.

SELECTING A QUALIFIED VET

Your selection of a veterinarian should be based not only upon his personality and abilities with small dogs but also upon his convenience to your home. You require a veterinarian who is close because you might have emergencies or need to make multiple visits for treatments. You want a vet who has services that you might require such as boarding, tattooing and grooming, as well as sophisticated pet supplies and a good reputation for ability and responsiveness. There is nothing more frustrating than having to wait a day or more to get a response from your veterinarian.

All veterinarians are licensed

Your Pom's best friend throughout his life—next to you, of course— will be his vet.

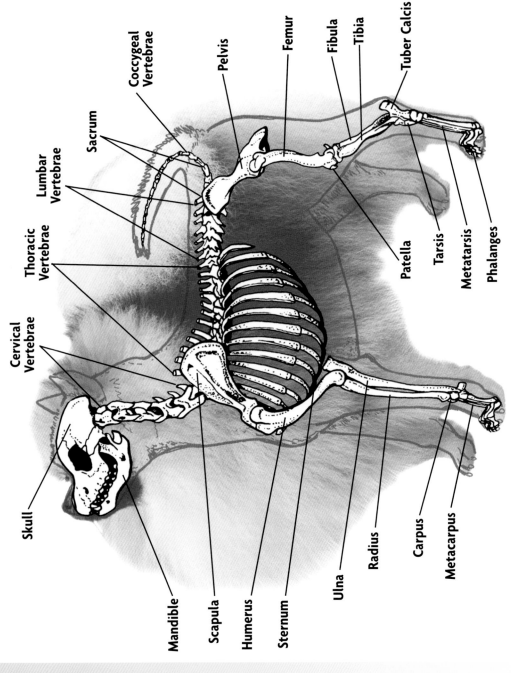

Coccygeal Vertebrae
Pelvis
Femur
Fibula
Tibia
Tuber Calcis
Sacrum
Lumbar Vertebrae
Thoracic Vertebrae
Patella
Tarsis
Metatarsis
Phalanges
Cervical Vertebrae
Skull
Mandible
Scapula
Humerus
Sternum
Ulna
Radius
Carpus
Metacarpus

Skeletal Structure of the Pomeranian

and their diplomas and/or certificates should be displayed in their waiting rooms. There are, however, many veterinary specialties that require further studies and internships. There are specialists in heart problems (veterinary cardiologists), skin problems (veterinary dermatologists), teeth and gum problems (veterinary dentists), eye problems (veterinary ophthalmologists) and x-rays (veterinary radiologists), and vets who have specialties in bones, muscles or certain organs. Most veterinarians do routine surgery such as neutering, stitching up wounds and docking tails for those breeds in which such is required for show purposes. When the problem affecting your dog is serious, it is not unusual or impudent to get another medical opinion, although it is always courteous to advise the vets concerned about this. You might also want to compare costs among several

Breakdown of Veterinary Income by Category

2%	Dentistry
4%	Radiology
12%	Surgery
15%	Vaccinations
19%	Laboratory
23%	Examinations
25%	Medicines

veterinarians. Sophisticated health care and veterinary services can be very costly. Don't be bashful about discussing these costs with your veterinarian or his staff. It is not infrequent that important decisions are based upon financial considerations.

A typical vet's income, categorized according to services performed. This survey dealt with small-animal (pets) practices.

PREVENTATIVE MEDICINE
It is much easier, less costly and more effective to practice preventative medicine than to fight bouts of illness and disease. Properly bred puppies come from parents that were selected based upon their genetic-disease profiles. Their mothers should have been vaccinated, free of all internal and external parasites and properly nourished. For these reasons, a visit to the veterinarian who cared for the dam is recommended. The dam can pass on disease resistance to her puppies, which can

NEUTERING/SPAYING
Male dogs are castrated. The operation removes both testicles and requires that the dog be anesthetized. Recovery takes about one week. Females are spayed; in this operation, the uterus (womb) and both of the ovaries are removed. This is major surgery, also carried out under general anesthesia, and it usually takes a bitch two weeks to recover.

Your veterinarian should be consulted as soon as you acquire your Pom pup to evaluate the pup's health at the time of purchase.

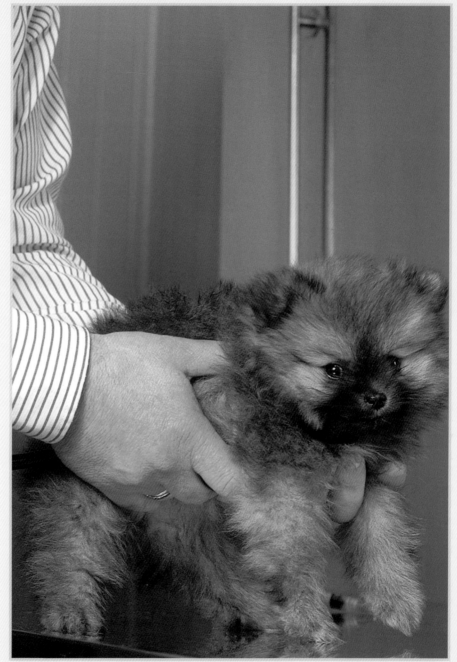

HEALTH AND VACCINATION SCHEDULE

AGE IN WEEKS:	6TH	8TH	10TH	12TH	14TH	16TH	20-24TH	52ND
Worm Control	✔	✔	✔	✔	✔	✔	✔	
Neutering								✔
Heartworm		✔			✔	✔	✔	
Parvovirus	✔		✔		✔		✔	✔
Distemper		✔		✔		✔		✔
Hepatitis		✔		✔		✔		✔
Leptospirosis								✔
Parainfluenza	✔		✔		✔			✔
Dental Examination		✔					✔	✔
Complete Physical		✔					✔	✔
Coronavirus				✔			✔	✔
Canine Cough	✔							
Hip Dysplasia								✔
Rabies							✔	

Vaccinations are not instantly effective. It takes about two weeks for the dog's immune system to develop antibodies. Most vaccinations require annual booster shots. Your vet should guide you in this regard.

last for eight to ten weeks. She can also pass on parasites and many infections. That's why you should learn as much about the dam and her health as possible.

WEANING TO FIVE MONTHS OLD
Puppies should be weaned by the time they are about two months old. A puppy that remains for *at least* eight weeks with his mother and littermates usually adapts better to other dogs and people later in his life.

Sometimes new owners have their puppy examined by a veterinarian immediately, unless the pup is tired from the ride home. In that case, an appointment should be arranged for the next day.

The puppy will have his teeth examined and have his skeletal conformation and general health checked prior to certification by the veterinarian. Puppies in certain breeds have problems with their kneecaps, cataracts and other eye problems, heart murmurs and undescended testicles. They may also have personality problems and your veterinarian might have training in temperament evaluation.

VACCINATION SCHEDULING
Most vaccinations are given by injection and should only be done by a veterinarian. Both he and you should keep a record of the date of the injection, the identification

Recognizing a Sick Dog

Unlike colicky babies and cranky children, our canine charges cannot tell us when they are feeling ill. Therefore, there are a number of signs that owners can identify to know that their dogs are not feeling well.

Take note for physical manifestations such as:

- unusual, bad odor, including bad breath
- excessive shedding
- wax in the ears, chronic ear irritation
- oily, flaky, dull haircoat
- mucus, tearing or similar discharge in the eyes
- fleas or mites
- mucus in stool, diarrhea
- sensitivity to petting or handling
- licking at paws, scratching face, etc.

Keep an eye out for behavioral changes as well including:

- lethargy, idleness
- lack of patience or general irritability
- lack of appetite
- phobias (fear of people, loud noises, etc.)
- strange behavior, suspicion, fear
- coprophagia
- more frequent barking
- whimpering, crying

Get Well Soon

You don't need a DVM to provide good TLC to your sick or recovering dog, but you do need to pay attention to some details that normally wouldn't bother him. The following tips will aid Fido's recovery and get him back on his paws again:

- Keep his space free of irritating smells, like heavy perfumes and air fresheners.
- Rest is the best medicine! Avoid harsh lighting that will prevent your dog from sleeping. Shade him from bright sunlight during the day and dim the lights in the evening.
- Keep the noise level down. Animals are more sensitive to sound when they are sick.

- Be attentive to any necessary temperature adjustments. A dog with a fever needs a cool room and cold liquids. A bitch that is whelping or recovering from surgery will be more comfortable in a warm room, consuming warm liquids and food.
- You wouldn't send a sick child back to school early, so don't rush your dog back into a full routine until he seems absolutely ready.

of the vaccine and the amount given. Some vets give a first vaccination at eight weeks, but most dog breeders prefer to wait until about ten weeks because of the risk of negating any antibodies passed on by the dam. The vaccination scheduling is usually based on a 15-day cycle. You must take your vet's advice as to when to vaccinate as this may differ according to the vaccine used.

Most vaccinations immunize your puppy against viruses. The usual vaccines contain immunizing doses of several different viruses such as distemper, parvovirus, parainfluenza and hepatitis. There are other vaccines available when the puppy is at risk. You should rely upon professional advice. This is especially true for the booster-shot program. Most vaccination programs require a booster when the puppy is a year old and once a year thereafter. In some cases, circumstances may require more or less frequent immunizations. Canine cough, more formally known as tracheobronchitis, is treated with a vaccine that is sprayed into the

DISEASE REFERENCE CHART

	What is it?	What causes it?	Symptoms
Leptospirosis	Severe disease that affects the internal organs; can be spread to people.	A bacterium, which is often carried by rodents, that enters through mucous membranes and spreads quickly throughout the body.	Range from fever, vomiting and loss of appetite in less severe cases to shock, irreversible kidney damage and possibly death in most severe cases.
Rabies	Potentially deadly virus that infects warm-blooded mammals.	Bite from a carrier of the virus, mainly wild animals.	1st stage: dog exhibits change in behavior, fear. 2nd stage: dog's behavior becomes more aggressive. 3rd stage: loss of coordination, trouble with bodily functions.
Parvovirus	Highly contagious virus, potentially deadly.	Ingestion of the virus, which is usually spread through the feces of infected dogs.	Most common: severe diarrhea. Also vomiting, fatigue, lack of appetite.
Canine cough	Contagious respiratory infection.	Combination of types of bacteria and virus. Most common: *Bordetella bronchiseptica* bacteria and parainfluenza virus.	Chronic cough.
Distemper	Disease primarily affecting the respiratory and nervous system.	Virus that is related to the human measles virus.	Mild symptoms such as fever, lack of appetite and mucous secretion progress to evidence of brain damage, "hard pad."
Hepatitis	Virus primarily affecting the liver.	Canine adenovirus type I (CAV-1). Enters system when dog breathes in particles.	Lesser symptoms include listlessness, diarrhea, vomiting. More severe symptoms include "blue-eye" (clumps of virus in eye).
Coronavirus	Virus resulting in digestive problems.	Virus is spread through infected dog's feces.	Stomach upset evidenced by lack of appetite, vomiting, diarrhea.

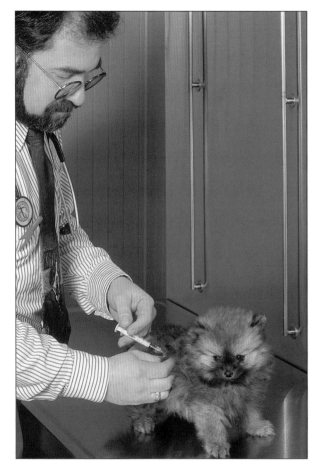

opinions differ regarding the best age at which to have this done. Most professionals advise neutering the puppy. Neutering has proven to be extremely beneficial to both male and female dogs. Besides eliminating the possibility of pregnancy, it inhibits (but does not prevent) breast cancer in bitches and prostate cancer in male dogs.

OVER ONE YEAR OF AGE

Once a year, your grown dog should visit the vet for an examination and vaccination boosters. Some vets recommend blood tests, thyroid level check and dental evaluation to accompany these annual visits. A thorough clinical evaluation by the vet can provide critical background information for your dog. Blood tests are often performed at one year of age, and dental examinations around the third or fourth birthday. In the long run, quality preventative care for your pet can save money, teeth and lives.

Embark on your Pom puppy's inoculation schedule with the assistance of your vet. Follow the instructions of the vet and keep careful records of all injections administered.

dog's nostrils. Canine cough is usually included in routine vaccination, but this is often not so effective as for other major diseases.

FIVE MONTHS TO ONE YEAR OF AGE

Unless you intend to breed or show your dog, neutering the puppy is recommended. Discuss this with your veterinarian, as

VACCINE ALLERGIES

Vaccines do not work all the time. Sometimes dogs are allergic to them and many times the antibodies, which are supposed to be stimulated by the vaccine, just are not produced. You should keep your dog in the veterinary clinic for an hour after he is vaccinated to be sure there are no allergic reactions.

SKIN PROBLEMS

Veterinarians are consulted by dog owners for skin problems more than any other group of diseases or maladies. Dogs' skin is almost as sensitive as human skin and both suffer almost the same ailments (though the occurrence of acne in dogs is rare!). For this reason, veterinary dermatology has developed into a specialty practiced by many veterinarians.

Since many skin problems have visual symptoms that are almost identical, it requires the skill of an experienced veterinary dermatologist to identify and cure many of the more severe skin disorders. Pet shops sell many treatments for skin problems but most of the treatments are directed at symptoms and not the underlying problem(s). If your dog is suffering from a skin disorder, you should seek professional assistance as quickly as possible. As with all diseases, the earlier a problem is identified and treated, the more likely is a complete recovery and/or cure.

ALOPECIA

Some Pomeranians are prone to skin disease, often a form of alopecia, indicated by a loss of hair. A lamb and rice diet, coupled with additional vitamin E intake, can be beneficial for this. Hair loss in the Pomeranian can be a hereditary problem, thought to be a hereditary growth-

DENTAL HEALTH

A dental examination is in order when the dog is between six months and one year of age so that any permanent teeth that have erupted incorrectly can be corrected. It is important to begin a brushing routine at home, using dental-care products made for dogs, such as small toothbrushes and specially formulated toothpaste. Durable nylon and safe edible chews should be a part of your puppy's arsenal for good health, good teeth and pleasant breath. The vast majority of dogs three to four years old and older has diseases of the gums from lack of dental attention. Using the various types of dental chews can be very effective in controlling dental plaque.

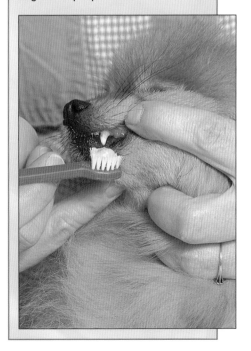

hormone deficiency. Often it affects the rear end and tail in Pomeranians. It is seen more often in males, though occasionally females are affected. This problem frequently appears at two to three years of age, so it is not possible to ascertain whether it is present when purchasing a puppy. A term often used for hair loss in the Pomeranian is "black skin disease."

Hypothyroidism is another very serious problem that can affect coat growth and cause hair loss. This can occur in many breeds so should be investigated and not dismissed.

ALLERGIES
Like all other breeds, Pomeranians can also be affected by allergies, but they can often be kept under control with a carefully consid-

The Eyes Have It!

Eye disease is more prevalent among dogs than most people think, ranging from slight infections that are easily treated to serious complications that can lead to permanent sight loss. Eye diseases need veterinary attention in their early stages to prevent irreparable damage. This list provides descriptions of some common eye diseases:

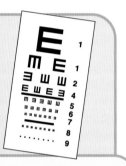

Cataracts: Symptoms are white or gray discoloration of the eye lens and pupil, which causes fuzzy or completely obscured vision. Surgical treatment is required to remove the damaged lens and replace it with an artificial one.
Conjunctivitis: An inflammation of the mucous membrane that lines the eye socket, leaving the eyes red and puffy with excessive discharge. This condition is easily treated with antibiotics.
Corneal damage: The cornea is the transparent covering of the iris and pupil. Injuries are difficult to detect, but manifest themselves in surface abnormality, redness, pain and discharge. Most infections of the cornea are treated with antibiotics and require immediate medical attention.
Dry eye: This condition is caused by deficient production of tears that lubricate and protect the eye surface. A telltale sign is yellow-green discharge. Left undiagnosed, your dog will experience considerable pain, infections and possibly blindness. Dry eye is commonly treated with antibiotics, although more advanced cases may require surgery.
Glaucoma: This is caused by excessive fluid pressure in the eye. Symptoms are red eyes, gray or blue discoloration, pain, enlarged eyeballs and loss of vision. Antibiotics sometimes help, but surgery may be needed.

THE SAME ALLERGIES
Chances are that you and your dog will have the same allergies. Your allergies are readily recognizable and usually easily treated. Your dog's allergies may be masked.

ered diet. The allergy is often noticed as "hot spots" on the skin, despite there being no sign of external parasites. Your vet can suggest a diet to suit skin troubles. It is often extremely difficult to ascertain the cause of the allergy. There are many possibilities, ranging from the sitting-room carpet, the shampoo used when bathing and, quite frequently, certain grasses and molds. In cases of skin allergy, it is a good idea to change shampoo, conditioning rinse and any other coat sprays used, for these are perhaps the easiest items to eliminate before looking further if necessary. It goes without saying that your Pomeranian must be kept free of external parasites such as fleas.

HEREDITARY SKIN DISORDERS
Veterinary dermatologists are currently researching a number of skin disorders that are believed to have a hereditary basis. These inherited diseases are transmitted by both parents, who appear (phenotypically) normal but have a recessive gene for the disease, meaning that they carry, but are not affected by, the disease. These diseases pose serious problems to breeders because in some instances there is no method of identifying carriers. Often the secondary diseases associated with these skin conditions are even more debilitating than the skin disorder, including cancers and respiratory problems.

Among the known hereditary skin disorders, for which the mode of inheritance is known, are acrodermatitis, cutaneous asthenia (Ehlers-Danlos syndrome), sebaceous adenitis, cyclic hematopoiesis, dermatomyositis, IgA deficiency, color dilution alopecia and nodular dermatofibrosis. Cyclic hematopoiesis, also know as gray Collie syndrome, has been reported in some Poms. Affected pups are born with a silver-gray haircoat, a light-colored nose and weaker frames. Problems can ensue by eight weeks of age. Some of these disorders are limited to one or two breeds and others affect a large number of breeds. All inherited diseases must be diagnosed and treated by a veterinary specialist.

PARASITE BITES
Many of us are allergic to insect bites. The bites itch, erupt and may even become infected. Dogs have the same reaction to fleas, ticks and/or mites. When an insect lands on you, you have the chance to whisk it away with your

hand. Unfortunately, when your dog is bitten by a flea, tick or mite, he can only scratch it away or bite it. By the time the dog has been bitten, the parasite has done some of its damage. It may also have laid eggs to cause further problems in the near future. The itching from parasite bites is probably due to the saliva injected into the site when the parasite sucks the dog's blood.

Auto-Immune Skin Conditions

Auto-immune skin conditions are commonly referred to as being allergic to yourself, while allergies are usually inflammatory reactions to an outside stimulus. Auto-immune diseases cause serious damage to the tissues that are involved.

The best known auto-immune disease is lupus, which affects people as well as dogs. The symptoms are variable and may affect the kidneys, bones, blood chemistry and skin. It can be fatal to both dogs and humans, though it is not thought to be transmissible. It is usually successfully treated with cortisone, prednisone or a similar corticosteroid, but extensive use of these drugs can have harmful side effects.

Airborne Allergies

Just as humans have hay fever, rose fever and other fevers from which they suffer during the pollinating season, many dogs suffer from the same allergies. When the pollen count is high, your dog might suffer, but don't expect him to sneeze and have a runny nose as a human would. Dogs react to pollen allergies the same way they react to fleas—they scratch and bite themselves.

Dogs, like humans, can be tested for allergens. Discuss the testing with your veterinary dermatologist.

BE CAREFUL WHERE YOU WALK YOUR DOG

Dogs who have been exposed to lawns sprayed with herbicides have double and triple the rate of malignant lymphoma. Suburban dogs are especially at risk, as they are exposed to manicured lawns and gardens. Dogs perspire and absorb through their footpads. Be careful where your dog walks and always avoid any area that appears yellowed from chemical overspray. These chemicals are not good for you, either!

FOOD PROBLEMS

FOOD ALLERGIES

Dogs are allergic to many foods that may be best-sellers and highly recommended by breeders and veterinarians. Changing the brand of food that you buy may not eliminate the problem if the element to which the dog is allergic is contained in the new brand.

Recognizing a food allergy is difficult. Humans vomit or have rashes when they eat a food to which they are allergic. Dogs neither vomit nor (usually) develop a rash. They react in the same manner as they do to an airborne or flea allergy: they itch, scratch and bite. This makes the diagnosis extremely difficult. While pollen allergies and parasite bites are usually seasonal, food allergies are year-round.

FOOD INTOLERANCE

Food intolerance is the inability of the dog to completely digest certain foods. For example, puppies that may have done very well on their mother's milk may not do well on cow's milk, which of course is common in most homes. The result of this food intolerance may be loose bowels, passing gas and stomach pains. These are the only obvious symptoms of food intolerance and that makes diagnosis difficult.

TREATING FOOD PROBLEMS

It is possible to handle food allergies and food intolerance yourself. Put your dog on a diet that he has never had. Obviously, if he has never eaten this new food he can't yet have been allergic or intolerant of it. Start with a single ingredient that is not in the dog's diet at the present time. Ingredients like chopped beef or chicken are common in dog's diets, so try something different like fish, lamb or some other source of protein. Keep the dog on this diet (with no additives) for a month. If the symptoms of food allergy or intolerance disappear, chances are your dog has a food allergy.

Don't think that the single ingredient cured the problem. You still must find a suitable diet and ascertain which ingredient in the old diet was objectionable. This is most easily done by adding ingredients to the new diet one at a time. Let the dog stay on the modified diet for a month before you add another ingredient. Eventually, you will determine the ingredient that caused the adverse reaction.

An alternative method is to carefully study the ingredients in the diet to which your dog is allergic or intolerant. Identify the main ingredient in this diet and eliminate the main ingredient by buying a different food that does not have that ingredient. Keep experimenting until the symptoms disappear after one month on the new diet.

A male dog flea, *Ctenocephalides canis.*

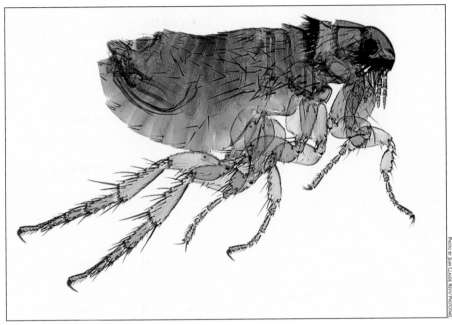

EXTERNAL PARASITES

FLEAS

Of all the problems to which dogs are prone, none is more well known and frustrating than fleas. Flea infestation is relatively simple to cure but difficult to prevent. Parasites that are harbored inside the body are a bit more difficult to eradicate but they are easier to control.

To control flea infestation, you have to understand the flea's life cycle. Fleas are often thought of as a summertime problem, but centrally heated homes have changed the patterns and fleas can be found at any time of the year. The most effective method of flea control is a two-stage approach: one stage to kill the adult fleas, and the other to control the development of pre-adult fleas. Unfortunately, no single active ingredient is effective against all stages of the life cycle.

FLEA KILLER CAUTION— "POISON"

Flea-killers are poisonous. You should not spray these toxic chemicals on areas of a dog's body that he licks, including his genitals and his face. Flea killers taken internally are a better answer, but check with your vet in case internal therapy is not advised for your dog.

LIFE CYCLE STAGES

During its life, a flea will pass through four life stages: egg, larva, pupa or nymph and adult. The adult stage is the most visible and irritating stage of the flea life cycle, and this is why the majority of flea-control products concentrate on this stage. The fact is that adult fleas account for only 1% of the total flea population, and the other 99% exist in pre-adult stages, i.e., eggs, larvae and nymphs. The pre-adult stages are barely visible to the naked eye.

THE LIFE CYCLE OF THE FLEA

Eggs are laid on the dog, usually in quantities of about 20 or 30, several times a day. The adult female flea must have a blood meal before each egg-laying session. When first laid, the eggs will cling to the dog's hair, as the eggs are still moist. However, they will quickly dry out and fall from the dog, especially if the dog moves around or scratches. Many eggs will fall off in the dog's favorite area or an area in which he spends a lot of time, such as his bed.

Once the eggs fall from the dog onto the carpet or furniture, they will hatch into larvae. This takes from one to ten days. Larvae are not particularly mobile and will usually travel only a few inches from where they hatch. However, they do have a tendency to move away from bright light and heavy

EN GARDE:
CATCHING FLEAS OFF GUARD!
Consider the following ways to arm yourself against fleas:
- Add a small amount of pennyroyal or eucalyptus oil to your dog's bath. These natural remedies repel fleas.
- Supplement your dog's food with fresh garlic (minced or grated) and a hearty amount of brewer's yeast, both of which ward off fleas.
- Use a flea comb on your dog daily. Submerge fleas in a cup of bleach to kill them quickly.
- Confine the dog to only a few rooms to limit the spread of fleas in the home.
- Vacuum daily...and get all of the crevices! Dispose of the bag every few days until the problem is under control.
- Wash your dog's bedding daily. Cover cushions where your dog sleeps with towels, and wash the towels often.

traffic—under furniture and behind doors are common places to find high quantities of flea larvae.

The flea larvae feed on dead organic matter, including adult flea feces, until they are ready to change into adult fleas. Fleas will usually remain as larvae for around seven days. After this period, the larvae will pupate into protective pupae. While inside the pupae, the larvae will undergo metamorphosis and change into adult fleas. This can take as little time as a few days, but the adult fleas can remain inside the pupae waiting to hatch for up to two years. The pupae are signaled to hatch by certain stimuli, such as physical pressure—the pupae's being stepped on, heat from an animal's lying on the pupae or increased carbon-dioxide levels and vibrations—indicating that a suitable host is available.

Once hatched, the adult flea must feed within a few days. Once the adult flea finds a host, it will not leave voluntarily. It only becomes dislodged by grooming or the host animal's scratching.

The adult flea will remain on the host for the duration of its life unless forcibly removed.

TREATING THE ENVIRONMENT AND THE DOG

Treating fleas should be a two-pronged attack. First, the environment needs to be treated; this includes carpets and furniture, especially the dog's bedding and areas underneath furniture. The environment should be treated with a household spray containing an Insect Growth Regulator (IGR) and an insecticide to kill the adult fleas. Most IGRs are effective against eggs and larvae; they actually mimic the fleas' own hormones and stop the eggs and larvae from developing into adult fleas. There are currently no treatments available to attack the pupa stage of the life cycle, so the adult insecticide is used to kill the newly hatched adult fleas before they find a host. Most IGRs are active for many months, while

A scanning electron micrograph of a dog or cat flea, *Ctenocephalides*, magnified more than 100x. This image has been colorized for effect.

THE LIFE CYCLE OF THE FLEA

Adult

Egg

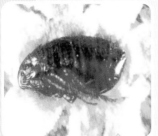

**Pupa
or
Nymph**

Larva

Fleas have been around for millions of years and have adapted to changing host animals. They are able to go through a complete life cycle in less than one month or they can extend their lives to almost two years by remaining as pupae or cocoons. They do not need blood or any other food for up to 20 months.

INSECT GROWTH REGULATOR (IGR)

Two types of products should be used when treating fleas—a product to treat the pet and a product to treat the home. Adult fleas represent less than 1% of the flea population. The pre-adult fleas (eggs, larvae and pupae) represent more than 99% of the flea population and are found in the environment; it is in the case of pre-adult fleas that products containing an Insect Growth Regulator (IGR) should be used in the home.

IGRs are a new class of compounds used to prevent the development of insects. They do not kill the insect outright, but instead use the insect's biology against it to stop it from completing its growth. Products that contain methoprene are the world's first and leading IGRs. Used to control fleas and other insects, this type of IGR will stop flea larvae from developing and protect the house for up to seven months.

The American dog tick, *Dermacentor variabilis*, is probably the most common tick found on dogs. Look at the strength in its eight legs! No wonder it's hard to detach them.

adult insecticides are only active for a few days.

When treating with a household spray, it is a good idea to vacuum before applying the product. This stimulates as many pupae as possible to hatch into adult fleas. The vacuum cleaner should also be treated with an insecticide to prevent the eggs and larvae that have been collected in the vacuum bag from hatching.

The second stage of treatment is to apply an adult insecticide to the dog. Traditionally, this would be in the form of a collar or a spray, but more recent innovations include digestible insecticides that poison the fleas when they ingest the dog's blood. Alternatively, there are drops that, when placed on the back of the dog's neck, spread throughout the hair and skin to kill adult fleas.

TICKS

Though not as common as fleas, ticks are found all over the tropical and temperate world. They don't bite, like fleas; they harpoon. They dig their sharp proboscis (nose) into the dog's

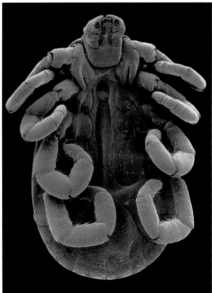

S.E.M. BY DR. DENNIS KUNKEL, UNIVERSITY OF HAWAII

skin and drink the blood. Their only food and drink is dog's blood. Dogs can get Lyme disease, Rocky Mountain spotted fever, tick bite paralysis and many other diseases from ticks. They may live where fleas are found and they like to hide in cracks or seams in walls. They are controlled the same way fleas are controlled.

The American dog tick, *Dermacentor variabilis*, may well be the most common dog tick in many geographical areas, especially those areas where the climate is hot and humid. Most dog ticks have life expectancies of a week to six months, depending upon climatic conditions. They can neither jump nor fly, but they can crawl slowly and can range up to 16 feet to reach a sleeping or unsuspecting dog.

MITES

Just as fleas and ticks can be problematic for your dog, mites can also lead to an itchy nuisance. Microscopic in size, mites are related to ticks and generally take up permanent residence on their host animal—in this case, your dog! The term *mange* refers to any infestation caused by one of the mighty mites, of which there are six varieties that concern owners.

Demodex mites cause a condition known as demodicosis

DEER-TICK CROSSING

The great outdoors may be fun for your dog, but it also is a home to dangerous ticks. Deer ticks carry a bacterium known as *Borrelia burgdorferi* and are most active in the autumn and spring. When infections are caught early, penicillin and tetracycline are effective antibiotics, but, if left untreated, the bacteria may cause neurological, kidney and cardiac problems as well as long-term trouble with walking and painful joints.

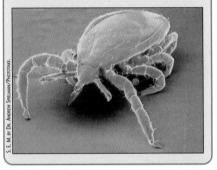

S. E. M. BY DR. ANDREW SPIELMAN/PHOTOTAKE.

PHOTO BY DR. DENNIS KUNKEL, UNIVERSITY OF HAWAII.

The head of an American dog tick, *Dermacentor variabilis*, enlarged and colorized for effect.

The mange mite, *Psoroptes bovis*, can infest cattle and other domestic animals.

PHOTO BY JAMES HAYDEN/YOAV/PHOTOTAKE

(sometimes called red mange or follicular mange), in which the mites live in the dog's hair follicles and sebaceous glands in larger-than-normal numbers. This type of mange is commonly passed from the dam to her puppies and usually shows up on the puppies' muzzles, though demodicosis is not transferable from one normal dog to another. Most dogs recover from this type of mange without any treatment, though topical therapies are commonly prescribed by the vet.

The *Cheyletiellosis* mite is the

Human lice look like dog lice; the two are closely related.

PHOTO BY DWIGHT R. KUHN.

hook-mouthed culprit associated with "walking dandruff," a condition that affects dogs as well as cats and rabbits. This mite lives on the surface of the animal's skin and is readily transferable through direct or indirect contact with an affected animal. The dandruff is present in the form of scaly skin, which may or may not be itchy. If not treated, this mange can affect a whole kennel of dogs and can be spread to humans as well.

The *Sarcoptes* mite causes intense itching on the dog in the form of a condition known as scabies or sarcoptic mange. The cycle of the *Sarcoptes* mite lasts about three weeks, and the mites live in the top layer of the dog's skin (epidermis), preferably in areas with little hair. Scabies is highly contagious and can be passed to humans. Sometimes an allergic reaction to the mite worsens the severe itching associated with sarcoptic mange.

Ear mites, *Otodectes cynotis,* lead to otodectic mange, which most commonly affects the outer ear canal of the dog, though other areas can be affected as well. Dogs with ear-mite infestation commonly scratch at their ears, causing further irritation, and shake their heads. Dark brown droppings in the outer ear confirm the diagnosis. Your vet can prescribe a treatment to flush out the ears and kill any eggs in the ears. A complete month of treatment is necessary to cure the mange.

Two other mites, less common in dogs, include *Dermanyssus gallinae* (the poultry or red mite) and *Eutrombicula alfreddugesi* (the North American mite associated with trombiculidiasis or chigger infestation). The poultry mite frequently lives on chickens, but can transfer to dogs who spend time near farm animals. Chigger

---

NOT A DROP TO DRINK
Never allow your dog to swim in polluted water or public areas where water quality can be suspect. Even perfectly clear water can harbor parasites, many of which can cause serious to fatal illnesses in canines. Areas inhabited by waterfowl and other wildlife are especially dangerous.

---

infestation affects dogs in the Central US who have exposure to woodlands. The types of mange caused by both of these mites are treatable by vets.

INTERNAL PARASITES
Most animals—fishes, birds and mammals, including dogs and humans—have worms and other parasites that live inside their bodies. According to Dr. Herbert R. Axelrod, the fish pathologist, there are two kinds of parasites: dumb and smart. The smart parasites live in peaceful cooperation with their hosts (symbiosis), while the dumb parasites kill their hosts. Most worm infections are relatively easy to control. If they are not controlled, they weaken the host dog to the point that other medical problems occur, but they do not kill the host as dumb parasites would.

The brown dog tick, *Rhipicephalus sanguineus,* is an uncommon but annoying tick found on dogs. PHOTO BY CAROLINA BIOLOGICAL SUPPLY/PHOTOTAKE.

DO NOT MIX
Never mix parasite-control products without first consulting your vet. Some products can become toxic when combined with others and can cause fatal consequences.

Photo by Carolina Biological Supply/Phototake

The roundworm *Rhabditis* can infect both dogs and humans.

ROUNDWORMS

Average-size dogs can pass 1,360,000 roundworm eggs every day. For example, if there were only 1 million dogs in the world, the world would be saturated with thousands of tons of dog feces. These feces would contain around 15,000,000,000 roundworm eggs.

Up to 31% of home yards and children's sand boxes in the US contain roundworm eggs.

Flushing dog's feces down the toilet is not a safe practice because the usual sewage treatments do not destroy roundworm eggs.

Infected puppies start shedding roundworm eggs at three weeks of age. They can be infected by their mother's milk.

The roundworm, *Ascaris lumbricoides*.

Photo by Dwight R. Kuhn

ROUNDWORMS

The roundworms that infect dogs are known scientifically as *Toxocara canis*. They live in the dog's intestines and shed eggs continually. It has been estimated that a dog produces about 6 or more ounces of feces every day. Each ounce of feces averages hundreds of thousands of roundworm eggs. There are no known areas in which dogs roam that do not contain roundworm eggs. The greatest danger of roundworms is that they infect people, too! It is wise to have your dog tested regularly for roundworms.

In young puppies, roundworms cause bloated bellies, diarrhea, coughing and vomiting, and are transmitted from the dam (through blood or milk). Affected puppies will not appear as animated as normal puppies. The worms appear spaghetti-like, measuring as long as 6 inches. Adult dogs can acquire roundworms through coprophagia (eating contaminated feces) or by killing rodents that carry roundworms.

Roundworm infection can kill puppies and cause severe problems in adults, as the hatched larvae travel to the lungs and trachea through the bloodstream. Cleanliness is the best preventative for roundworms. Always pick up after your dog and dispose of feces in appropriate receptacles.

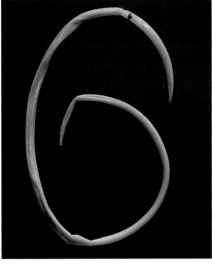

PHOTO BY DWIGHT R. KUHN.

HOOKWORMS

In the United States, dog owners have to be concerned about four different species of hookworm, the most common and most serious of which is *Ancylostoma caninum,* which prefers warm climates. The others are *Ancylostoma braziliense, Ancylostoma tubaeforme* and *Uncinaria stenocephala,* the latter of which is a concern to dogs living in the Northern US and Canada, as this species prefers cold climates. Hookworms are dangerous to humans as well as to dogs and cats, and can be the cause of severe anemia due to iron deficiency. The worm uses its teeth to attach itself to the dog's intestines and changes the site of its attachment about six times per day. Each time the worm

repositions itself, the dog loses blood and can become anemic. *Ancylostoma caninum* is the most likely of the four species to cause anemia in the dog.

Symptoms of hookworm infection include dark stools, weight loss, general weakness, pale coloration and anemia, as well as possible skin problems. Fortunately, hookworms are easily purged from the affected dog with a number of medications that have proven effective. Discuss these with your vet. Most heartworm preventatives include a hookworm insecticide as well.

Owners also must be aware that hookworms can infect humans, who can acquire the larvae through exposure to contaminated feces. Since the worms cannot complete their life cycle on a human, the worms simply infest the skin and cause irritation. This condition is known as cutaneous larva migrans syndrome. As a preventative, use disposable gloves or a "poop-scoop" to pick up your dog's droppings and prevent your dog (or neighborhood cats) from defecating in children's play areas.

The hookworm, *Ancylostoma caninum.*

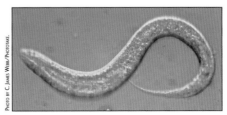

PHOTO BY C. JAMES WEBB/PHOTOTAKE.

The infective stage of the hookworm larva.

TAPEWORMS

Humans, rats, squirrels, foxes, coyotes, wolves and domestic dogs are all susceptible to tapeworm infection. Except in humans, tapeworms are usually not a fatal infection. Infected individuals can harbor 1,000 parasitic worms.

Tapeworms, like some other types of worm, are hermaphroditic, meaning male and female in the same worm.

If dogs eat infected rats or mice, or anything else infected with tapeworm, they get the tapeworm disease. One month after attaching to a dog's intestine, the worm starts shedding eggs. These eggs are infective immediately. Infective eggs can live for a few months without a host animal.

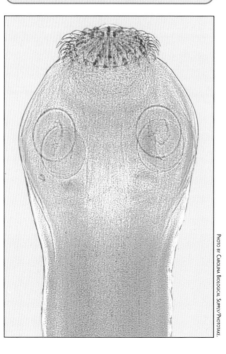

The head and rostellum (the round prominence on the scolex) of a tapeworm, which infects dogs and humans.

PHOTO BY CAROLINA BIOLOGICAL SUPPLY/PHOTOTAKE

TAPEWORMS

There are many species of tapeworm, all of which are carried by fleas! The most common tapeworm affecting dogs is known as *Dipylidium caninum*. The dog eats the flea and starts the tapeworm cycle. Humans can also be infected with tapeworms—so don't eat fleas! Fleas are so small that your dog could pass them onto your hands, your plate or your food and thus make it possible for you to ingest a flea that is carrying tapeworm eggs.

While tapeworm infection is not life-threatening in dogs (smart parasite!), it can be the cause of a very serious liver disease for humans. About 50% of the humans infected with *Echinococcus multilocularis*, a type of tapeworm that causes alveolar hydatid, perish.

WHIPWORMS

In North America, whipworms are counted among the most common parasitic worms in dogs. The whipworm's scientific name is *Trichuris vulpis*. These worms attach themselves in the lower parts of the intestine, where they feed. Affected dogs may only experience upset tummies, colic and diarrhea. These worms, however, can live for months or years in the dog, beginning their larval stage in the small intestine, spending their adult stage in the large intestine and finally passing infective eggs through the dog's feces. The only way to detect whipworms is through a fecal examination, though this is not always foolproof. Treatment for whipworms is tricky, due to the worms' unusual life-cycle pattern, and very often dogs are reinfected due to exposure to infective eggs on the ground. The whipworm eggs can survive in the environment for as long as five years, thus cleaning up droppings in your own backyard as well as in public places is absolutely essential for sanitation purposes and the health of your dog and others.

THREADWORMS
Though less common than roundworms, hookworms and the others previously mentioned, threadworms concern dog owners in the US where the climate is hot and humid. Living in the small intestine of the dog, this worm measures a mere 2 millimeters and is round in shape. Like that of the whipworm, the threadworm's life cycle is very complex and the eggs and larvae are passed through the feces. A deadly disease in humans, *Strongyloides* readily infects people, and handling feces is the most common means of transmission. Threadworms are most often seen in young puppies; bloody diarrhea and pneumonia are symptoms. Sick puppies must be isolated and treated immediately; vets recommend a follow-up treatment one month later.

HEARTWORM PREVENTATIVES

There are many heartworm preventatives on the market, many of which are sold at your veterinarian's office. These products can be given daily or monthly, depending on the manufacturer's instructions. All of these preventatives contain chemical insecticides directed at killing heartworms, which leads to some controversy among dog owners. In effect, heartworm preventatives are necessary evils, though you should determine how necessary based on your pet's lifestyle. There is no doubt that heartworm is a dreadful disease that threatens the lives of dogs. However, the likelihood of your dog's being bitten by an infected mosquito is slim in most places, and a mosquito-repellent (or an herbal remedy such as Wormwood or Black Walnut) is much safer for your dog and will not compromise his immune system (the way heartworm preventatives will). Should you decide to use the traditional preventative "medications," you can consider giving the pill every other or third month. Since the toxins in the pill will kill the heartworms at all stages of development, the pill would be effective in killing larvae, nymphs or adults, and it takes four months for the larvae to reach the adult stage. Thus, there is no rationale to poisoning the dog's system on a monthly basis. Lastly, do not give the pill during the winter months since there are no mosquitoes around to pass on their infection, unless you live in a tropical environment.

Life Cycle of the Heartworm

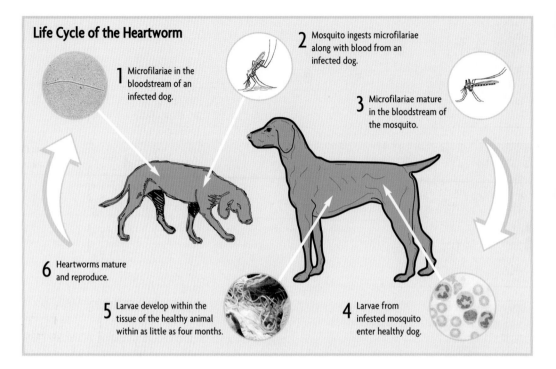

1 Microfilariae in the bloodstream of an infected dog.

2 Mosquito ingests microfilariae along with blood from an infected dog.

3 Microfilariae mature in the bloodstream of the mosquito.

6 Heartworms mature and reproduce.

5 Larvae develop within the tissue of the healthy animal within as little as four months.

4 Larvae from infested mosquito enter healthy dog.

HEARTWORMS

Heartworms are thin, extended worms up to 12 inches long, which live in a dog's heart and the major blood vessels surrounding it. Dogs may have up to 200 worms. Symptoms may be loss of energy, loss of appetite, coughing, the development of a pot belly and anemia.

Heartworms are transmitted by mosquitoes. The mosquito drinks the blood of an infected dog and takes in larvae with the blood. The larvae, called microfilariae, develop within the body of the mosquito and are passed on to the next dog bitten after the larvae mature. It takes two to three weeks for the larvae to develop to the infective stage within the body of the mosquito. Dogs are usually treated at about six weeks of age and maintained on a prophylactic dose given monthly.

Blood testing for heartworms is not necessarily indicative of how seriously your dog is infected. Although this is a dangerous disease, it is not easy for a dog to be infected. Discuss the various preventatives with your vet, as there are many different types now available. Together you can decide on a safe course of prevention for your dog.

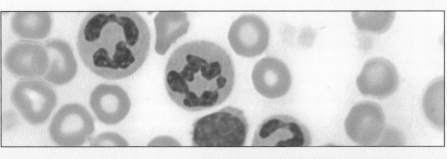

 PHOTO BY CAROLINA BIOLOGICAL SUPPLY/PHOTOTAKE.

Magnified heart-
worm larvae, *Diro-
filaria immitis.*

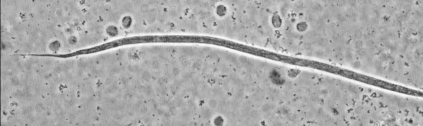

PHOTO BY J E HAYDEN, RBP/PHOTOTAKE.

Heartworm, *Diro-
filaria immitis.*

PHOTO BY JAMES E. HAYDEN, RBP/PHOTOTAKE.

The heart
of a dog infected
with canine heart-
worm, *Dirofilaria
immitis.*

HOMEOPATHY:
an alternative
to conventional
medicine

"Less is Most"

Using this principle, the strength of a homeopathic remedy is measured by the number of serial dilutions that were undertaken to create it. The greater the number of serial dilutions, the greater the strength of the homeopathic remedy. The potency of a remedy that has been made by making a dilution of 1 part in 100 parts (or 1/100) is 1c or 1cH. If this remedy is subjected to a series of further dilutions, each one being 1/100, a more dilute and stronger remedy is produced. If the remedy is diluted in this way six times, it is called 6c or 6cH. A dilution of 6c is 1 part in 1,000,000,000,000. In general, higher potencies in more frequent doses are better for acute symptoms and lower potencies in more infrequent doses are more useful for chronic, long-standing problems.

CURING OUR DOGS NATURALLY

Holistic medicine means treating the whole animal as a unique, perfect living being. Generally, holistic treatments do not suppress the symptoms that the body naturally produces, as do most medications prescribed by conventional doctors and vets. Holistic methods seek to cure disease by regaining balance and harmony in the patient's environment. Some of these methods include use of nutritional therapy, herbs, flower essences, aromatherapy, acupuncture, massage, chiropractic and, of course, the most popular holistic approach, homeopathy.

Homeopathy is a theory or system of treating illness with small doses of substances which, if administered in larger quantities, would produce the symptoms that the patient already has. This approach is often described as "like cures like." Although modern veterinary medicine is geared toward the "quick fix," homeopathy relies on the belief that, given the time, the body is able to heal itself and return to its natural, healthy state.

Choosing a remedy to cure a problem in our dogs is the difficult part of homeopathy. Consult with your vet for a professional diagnosis of your dog's symptoms. Often these symptoms require immediate conventional care. If your vet is willing and knowledgeable, you may attempt a homeopathic remedy. Be aware that cortisone prevents homeopathic remedies from working. There are hundreds of possibilities and combinations to cure many problems in dogs, from basic physical problems such as excessive shedding, fleas or other parasites, unattractive doggy odor, bad breath, upset tummy, obesity, dry, oily or dull coat, diarrhea, ear problems or eye discharge (including tears and dry or mucousy matter), to behavioral abnormalities such as fear of loud noises, habitual licking, poor appetite, excessive barking and various phobias. From alumina to zincum metallicum, the remedies span the planet and the imagination...from flowers and weeds to chemicals, insect droppings, diesel smoke and volcanic ash.

Using "Like to Treat Like"

Unlike conventional medicines that suppress symptoms, homeopathic remedies treat illnesses with small doses of substances that, if administered in larger quantities, would produce the symptoms that the patient already has. While the same homeopathic remedy can be used to treat different symptoms in different dogs, here are some interesting remedies and their uses.

Apis Mellifica
(made from honey bee venom) can be used for allergies or to reduce swelling that occurs in acutely infected kidneys.

Diesel Smoke
can be used to help control travel sickness.

Calcarea Fluorica
(made from calcium fluoride, which helps harden bone structure) can be useful in treating hard lumps in tissues.

Natrum Muriaticum
(made from common salt, sodium chloride) is useful in treating thin, thirsty dogs.

Nitricum Acidum
(made from nitric acid) is used for symptoms you would expect to see from contact with acids, such as lesions, especially where the skin joins the linings of body orifices or openings such as the lips and nostrils.

Symphytum
(made from the herb Knitbone, *Symphytum officianale*) is used to encourage bones to heal.

Urtica Urens
(made from the common stinging nettle) is used in treating painful, irritating rashes.

HOMEOPATHIC REMEDIES FOR YOUR DOG

Symptom/Ailment	Possible Remedy
ALLERGIES	Apis Mellifica 30c, Astacus Fluviatilis 6c, Pulsatilla 30c, Urtica Urens 6c
ALOPECIA	Alumina 30c, Lycopodium 30c, Sepia 30c, Thallium 6c
ANAL GLANDS (BLOCKED)	Hepar Sulphuris Calcareum 30c, Sanicula 6c, Silicea 6c
ARTHRITIS	Rhus Toxicodendron 6c, Bryonia Alba 6c
CATARACT	Calcarea Carbonica 6c, Conium Maculatum 6c, Phosphorus 30c, Silicea 30c
CONSTIPATION	Alumina 6c, Carbo Vegetabilis 30c, Graphites 6c, Nitricum Acidum 30c, Silicea 6c
COUGHING	Aconitum Napellus 6c, Belladonna 30c, Hyoscyamus Niger 30c, Phosphorus 30c
DIARRHEA	Arsenicum Album 30c, Aconitum Napellus 6c, Chamomilla 30c, Mercurius Corrosivus 30c
DRY EYE	Zincum Metallicum 30c
EAR PROBLEMS	Aconitum Napellus 30c, Belladonna 30c, Hepar Sulphuris 30c, Tellurium 30c, Psorinum 200c
EYE PROBLEMS	Borax 6c, Aconitum Napellus 30c, Graphites 6c, Staphysagria 6c, Thuja Occidentalis 30c
GLAUCOMA	Aconitum Napellus 30c, Apis Mellifica 6c, Phosphorus 30c
HEAT STROKE	Belladonna 30c, Gelsemium Sempervirens 30c, Sulphur 30c
HICCOUGHS	Cinchona Deficinalis 6c
HIP DYSPLASIA	Colocynthis 6c, Rhus Toxicodendron 6c, Bryonia Alba 6c
INCONTINENCE	Argentum Nitricum 6c, Causticum 30c, Conium Maculatum 30c, Pulsatilla 30c, Sepia 30c
INSECT BITES	Apis Mellifica 30c, Cantharis 30c, Hypericum Perforatum 6c, Urtica Urens 30c
ITCHING	Alumina 30c, Arsenicum Album 30c, Carbo Vegetabilis 30c, Hypericum Perforatum 6c, Mezerium 6c, Sulphur 30c
KENNEL COUGH	Drosera 6c, Ipecacuanha 30c
MASTITIS	Apis Mellifica 30c, Belladonna 30c, Urtica Urens 1m
MOTION SICKNESS	Cocculus 6c, Petroleum 6c
PATELLAR LUXATION	Gelsemium Sempervirens 6c, Rhus Toxicodendron 6c
PENIS PROBLEMS	Aconitum Napellus 30c, Hepar Sulphuris Calcareum 30c, Pulsatilla 30c, Thuja Occidentalis 6c
PUPPY TEETHING	Calcarea Carbonica 6c, Chamomilla 6c, Phytolacca 6c

First Aid at a Glance

Burns
Place the affected area under cool water; use ice if only a small area is burnt.

Bee stings/Insect bites
Apply ice to relieve swelling; antihistamine dosed properly.

Animal bites
Clean any bleeding area; apply pressure until bleeding subsides; go to the vet.

Spider bites
Use cold compress and a pressurized pack to inhibit venom's spreading.

Antifreeze poisoning
Induce vomiting with hydrogen peroxide. Seek *immediate* veterinary help!

Fish hooks
Removal best handled by vet; hook must be cut in order to remove.

Snake bites
Pack ice around bite; contact vet quickly; identify snake for proper antivenin.

Car accident
Move dog from roadway with blanket; seek veterinary aid.

Shock
Calm the dog; keep him warm; seek immediate veterinary help.

Nosebleed
Apply cold compress to the nose; apply pressure to any visible abrasion.

Bleeding
Apply pressure above the area; treat wound by applying a cotton pack.

Heat stroke
Submerge dog in cold bath; cool down with fresh air and water; go to the vet.

Frostbite/Hypothermia
Warm the dog with a warm bath, electric blankets or hot water bottles.

Abrasions
Clean the wound and wash out thoroughly with fresh water; apply antiseptic.

Remember: an injured dog may attempt to bite a helping hand from fear and confusion. Always muzzle the dog before trying to offer assistance.

Dog showing can be rewarding for children as well as adults. This young fellow is having a great time showing off his handsome Pomeranian.

SHOWING YOUR

POMERANIAN

When you purchase your Pomeranian, you will make it clear to the breeder whether you want one just as a lovable companion and pet, or if you hope to be buying a Pomeranian with show prospects. No reputable breeder will sell you a young puppy and tell you that it is *definitely* of show quality, for so much can go wrong during the early months of a puppy's development. If you plan to show, what

Like all other Toy breeds, the Pomeranian is examined on a table by the judge at dog shows. Hours of grooming sessions pay off doubly in the conformation ring!

you will hopefully have acquired is a puppy with "show potential."

To the novice, exhibiting a Pomeranian in the show ring may look easy, but it takes a lot of hard work and devotion to do top winning at a show such as the prestigious Westminster Kennel Club dog show, not to mention a little luck too!

The first concept that the canine novice learns when watching a dog show is that each dog first competes against members of his own breed. Once the judge has selected the best member of each breed (Best of Breed), provided that the show is judged on a Group system, that chosen dog will compete with other dogs in his group. Finally, the dogs

MEET THE AKC

The American Kennel Club is the main governing body of the dog sport in the United States. Founded in 1884, the AKC consists of 500 or more independent dog clubs plus 4,500 affiliate clubs, all of which follow the AKC rules and regulations. Additionally, the AKC maintains a registry for pure-bred dogs in the US and works to preserve the integrity of the sport and its continuation in the country. Over 1,000,000 dogs are registered each year, representing about 150 recognized breeds. There are over 15,000 competitive events held annually for which over 2,000,000 dogs enter to participate. Dogs compete to earn over 40 different titles, from Champion to Companion Dog to Master Agility Champion.

chosen first in each group will compete for Best in Show.

The second concept that you must understand is that the dogs are not actually compared against one another. The judge compares each dog against his breed standard, the written description of the ideal specimen that is approved by the American Kennel Club (AKC). While some early breed standards were indeed based on specific dogs that were famous or popular, many dedicated enthusiasts say that a perfect specimen, as described in the standard, has never walked into a show ring, has never been bred and, to the woe of dog breeders around the globe, does not exist. Breeders attempt to get as close to this ideal as possible with every litter, but theoretically the "perfect" dog is so elusive that it is impossible. (And if the "perfect" dog were born, breeders and judges would never agree that it was indeed "perfect.")

If you are interested in exploring the world of dog showing, your best bet is to join your local breed club or the national parent club, which is the American Pomeranian Club. These clubs often host both regional and national specialties, shows only for Pomeranians, which can include conformation as well as obedience and agility trials. Even if you have no intention of competing with your Pomeranian,

a specialty is like a festival for lovers of the breed who congregate to share their favorite topic: Pomeranians! Clubs also send out newsletters, and some organize training days and seminars in order that people may learn more about their chosen breed. To locate the breed club closest to you, contact the American Kennel Club, which furnishes the rules and regulations for all of these events plus general dog registration and other basic requirements of dog ownership.

The American Kennel Club offers three kinds of conformation shows: an all-breed show (for all AKC-recognized breeds); a specialty show (for one breed only, usually sponsored by the parent club) and a Group show (for all breeds in the Group).

For a dog to become an AKC champion of record, the dog must accumulate 15 points at the shows from at least three different judges, including two "majors." A "major" is defined as a three-, four- or five-point win, and the number of points per win is determined on the number of dogs entered in the show on that day. Depending on the breed, the number of points that are awarded varies. In a breed as popular as the Pomeranian, more dogs are needed to rack up the points. At any dog show, only one dog and one bitch of each breed can win points.

Some shows are less formal than others and prove to be as social as they are educational. These Pom owners are competing for Best of Breed.

Dog showing does not offer "co-ed" classes. Dogs and bitches never compete against each other in the classes. Non-champion dogs are called "class dogs" because they compete in one of five classes. Dogs are entered in a particular class depending on their age and previous show wins. To begin, there is the Puppy Class (for 6- to 9-month-olds and for 9- to 12-month-olds); this class is followed by the Novice Class (for dogs that have not won any first prizes except in the Puppy Class or three first prizes in the Novice Class and have not accumulated any points toward their champion title); the Bred-by-Exhibitor Class (for dogs handled by their breeders or handled by one of the breeder's immediate family); the American-bred Class (for dogs bred in the US!); and the Open Class (for any dog that is not a champion).

The judge at the show begins judging the Puppy Class, first dogs and then bitches, and proceeds through the classes. The judge places his winners first through fourth in each class. In the

Winners Class, the first-place winners of each class compete with one another to determine Winners Dog and Winners Bitch. The judge also places a Reserve Winners Dog and Reserve Winners Bitch, which could be awarded the points in the case of a disqualification. The Winners Dog and Winners Bitch, the two that are awarded the points for the breed, then compete with any champions of record entered in the show. The judge reviews the Winners Dog, Winners Bitch and all of the other champions (often called "specials") to select his Best of Breed. The Best of Winners is selected between the Winners Dog and Winners Bitch. Were one of these two to be selected Best of Breed, he or she would automatically be named Best of Winners as well. Finally the judge selects his Best of Opposite Sex to the Best of Breed winner.

At a Group show or all-breed show, the Best of Breed winners from each breed then compete against one another for Group One through Group Four. The judge compares each Best of Breed to his breed standard, and the dog that most closely lives up to the ideal for his breed is selected as Group One. Finally, all seven group winners (from the Toy Group, Sporting Group, Hound

This judge is evaluating two promising Poms. The handlers must keep the dogs alert and attentive while the judging is being conducted.

Group, etc.) compete for Best in Show.

To find out about dog shows in your area, you can subscribe to the American Kennel Club's monthly magazine, the *American Kennel Gazette* and the accompanying *Events Calendar*. You can also look in your local newspaper for advertisements for dog shows in your area or go on the Internet to the AKC's website, www.akc.org.

If your Pomeranian is six months of age or older and registered with the AKC, you can enter him in a dog show where the breed is offered classes. Provided that your Pomeranian does not have a disqualifying fault, he can compete. Only unaltered dogs can be entered in a dog show, so if you have spayed or neutered your Pomeranian, your dog cannot compete in conformation shows. The reason for this is simple. Dog shows are the main forum to prove which representatives in a breed are worthy of being bred. Only dogs that have achieved championships—the AKC "seal of approval" for quality in pure-bred dogs—-should be bred. Altered dogs, however, can participate in other AKC events such as obedience trials and the Canine Good Citizen program.

ENTERING A DOG SHOW

Before you actually step into the ring, you would be well advised to sit back and observe the judge's ring procedure. If it is your first time in the ring, stand back and study how the exhibitor in front of you is performing. The judge asks each handler to stand or "stack" the dog, hopefully showing the dog off to his best advantage. The judge will observe the dog from a distance and from different angles, and approach the dog to check his teeth, overall structure, alertness and muscle tone, as well as consider how well the dog "conforms" to the standard. Most importantly, the judge will have the exhibitor move the dog around the ring in some pattern that he should specify (always listen since some judges change their directions—and the judge is always right!). Finally, the judge will give the dog one last look before moving on to the next exhibitor.

If you are not in the top four in your class at your first show, do not be discouraged. Be patient and consistent, and you may eventually find yourself in a winning line-up. Remember that the winners were once in your shoes and have devoted many hours and much money to earn the placement. If you find that your dog is losing every time and never getting a nod, it may be time to consider a different dog sport or to just enjoy your Pomeranian as a pet. Parent clubs offer other events, such as agility, tracking, obedience, instinct tests and more, which may be of interest to the owner of a well-trained Pomeranian.

OBEDIENCE TRIALS

Obedience trials in the US trace back to the early 1930s when organized obedience training was developed to demonstrate how well dog and owner could work together. The pioneer of obedience trials is Mrs. Helen Whitehouse Walker, a Standard Poodle fancier, who designed a series of exercises after the Associated Sheep, Police Army Dog Society of Great Britain. Since the days of Mrs. Walker, obedience trials have grown by leaps and bounds, and today there are over 2,000 trials held in the US every year, with more than 100,000 dogs competing. Any AKC-registered dog can enter an obedience trial, regardless of conformational disqualifications or neutering.

Obedience trials are divided into three levels of progressive difficulty. At the first level, the Novice, dogs compete for the title Companion Dog (CD); at the intermediate level, the Open, dogs compete for the title Companion Dog Excellent (CDX); and at the advanced level, the Utility, dogs compete for the title Utility Dog (UD). Classes are sub-divided into "A" (for beginners) and "B" (for more experienced handlers). A perfect score at any level is 200, and a dog must score 170 or better

THE VICTORIAN POM

The Pomeranian is recognized by a number of registries, including the American Kennel Club, The Kennel Club, the United Kennel Club and the Canadian Kennel Club. However, the Fédération Cynologique Internationale (FCI) does not register the Pomeranian as a separate breed. They consider it to be the same breed as the German Zwergspitz, which was the breed imported (and renamed) by Queen Victoria. Over the years, the Pomeranian has become a more refined dog with a fuller, more abundant coat than his German cousin.

to earn a "leg," of which three are needed to earn the title. To earn points, the dog must score more than 50% of the available points in each exercise; the possible points range from 20 to 40.

Each level consists of a different set of exercises. In the Novice level, the dog must heel on- and off-leash, come, long sit, long down and stand for examination. These skills are the basic ones required for a well-behaved "Companion Dog." The Open level requires that the dog perform the same exercises above but without a leash for extended lengths of time, as well as retrieve a dumbbell, broad jump and drop on recall. In the Utility level, dogs must perform ten difficult exercises, including scent discrimination, hand signals for basic commands, directed jump and directed retrieve.

Once a dog has earned the UD title, he can compete with other proven obedience dogs for the coveted title of Utility Dog Excellent (UDX), which requires that the dog win "legs" in ten shows. Utility Dogs who earn "legs" in Open B and Utility B earn points toward their Obedience Trial Champion title. In 1977 the title Obedience Trial Champion (OTCh.) was established by the AKC. To become an OTCh., a dog needs to earn 100 points, which requires three first places in Open B and Utility under three different judges.

The Grand Prix of obedience trials, the AKC National Obedience Invitational gives qualifying Utility Dogs the chance to win the newest and highest title: National Obedience Champion (NOC). Only the top 25 ranked obedience dogs, plus any dog ranked in the top 3 in his breed, are allowed to compete.

AGILITY TRIALS
Having had its origins in the UK back in 1977, AKC agility had its official beginning in the US in August 1994, when the first licensed agility trials were held. The AKC allows all registered breeds (including Miscellaneous Class breeds) to participate, providing the dog is 12 months of age or older. Agility is designed so that the handler demonstrates how well the dog can work at his side. The handler directs his dog over an obstacle course that includes jumps as well as tires, the dog walk, weave poles, pipe tunnels, collapsed tunnels, etc. While working his way through the course, the dog must keep one eye and ear on the handler and the rest of his body on the course. The handler gives verbal and hand signals to guide the dog through the course.

Agility is great fun for dog and owner with many rewards for everyone involved. Interested owners should join a training club that has obstacles and experienced agility handlers who can introduce you and your dog to the "ropes" (and tires, tunnels, and so on).

INDEX

*Page numbers in **boldface** indicate illustrations.*

My Pomeranian

PUT YOUR PUPPY'S FIRST PICTURE HERE

Dog's Name _____

Date _____ Photographer _____